WHITE CITY RECOLLECTIONS

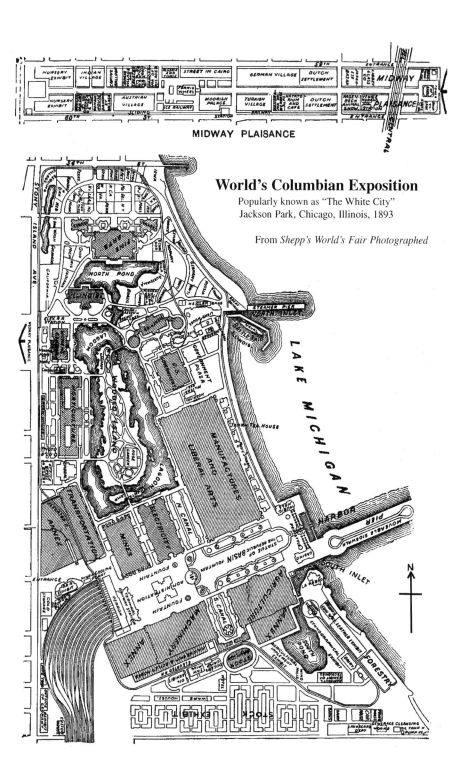

MIDWAY PLAISANCE

World's Columbian Exposition

Popularly known as "The White City"
Jackson Park, Chicago, Illinois, 1893

From *Shepp's World's Fair Photographed*

WHITE CITY RECOLLECTIONS

The Illustrated 1893 Diary

of

Friend Pitts Williams'

Trip to the

WORLD'S COLUMBIAN EXPOSITION

Edited and illustrated by

G. L. Dybwad and Joy V. Bliss

The Book Stops Here
Albuquerque, New Mexico

2003

Other books by Dybwad and Bliss

Annotated Bibliography: World's Columbian Exposition, Chicago 1893
James A. Michener, The Beginning Teacher and His Textbooks
Chicago Day at the World's Columbian Exposition
Annotated Bibliography: World's Columbian Exposition, Chicago 1893 Supplement
Dryden Pottery of Kansas and Arkansas

Dybwad, G. L., and Joy V. Bliss
White City Recollections : The Illustrated 1893 Diary of Friend Pitts
Williams' Trip to the World's Columbian Exposition

ISBN Number: 0-9631612-2-9
LCCN: 2003090233

Includes index, illustration source list, and bibliography
1. Williams, Friend Pitts, 1875–1939. 2. World's Columbian Exposition.
3. Chicago, Illinois 4. World's Fairs—American Expositions—1893.
I. Title.

The Book Stops Here, Publisher
1108 Rocky Point Court NE
Albuquerque, NM 87123-1952
Telephone: 505-296-9047
gldybwad@comcast.net
www.bookstopshere.com

First Edition

Front cover: Adapted from the chromolithographic cover of *The Youth's*
Companion : *World's Fair Number*, May 4, 1893.

Back cover: Adapted from a real photograph cabinet card of the Ferris
Wheel by Brisbois Photo Company, 1893.

Printed by BookMobile, St. Paul, Minnesota. Cover design by G. L. Dybwad.

The fifty-eight-page typescript diary of a trip to the World's Columbian Exposition, Chicago 1893, has light blue covers riveted at the top and "World's Fair" printed boldly in gilt on the front cover. 17 centimeters high x 21.

INTRODUCTION

An accurate and well-written diary exhibiting the now-quaint language of Victorian 1893 is the keystone of this book. We have added illustrations, turning the diary into a visual re-creation of the diarist's trip to the World's Columbian Exposition, popularly called "The White City" for the uniform white lead paint sprayed on the major buildings. Illustrations are taken from our 1893 reference library and closely match the views seen and described by the diarist. A source list for these illustrations begins on page 174.

The diary was not signed, but from its narrative we knew that the trip started on August 17, 1893, in Olean, New York, that the youth had just graduated from high school, and that he traveled to the fair with his father. We had assumed he was male, judging from the exhibits he found most appealing; and a contemporary Olean newspaper, which listed one father-son departure during the month of August confirmed this. It appeared on the very day the diary begins, August 17, 1893.

eral of Dr. E. S. Jackson.
Alderman A. I. Williams and son Friend P. Williams will leave to-day for a visit at Chicago and the Fair.
Miss Nettie Eaton of Laurel avenue,

Departure listing in the *Olean Daily Herald* for August 17, 1893. This announcement was also printed in the *Olean Evening Times* of August 17, 1893. (Courtesy of *Olean Times Herald*, Olean, New York)

The travelers were identified as Friend Pitts Williams and his father, Allan Irving Williams. Further details were learned through telephone calls to numerous New Yorkers with the "Williams" surname and through school and historical society records.

Finding Walter Le Grys, who joined the Williams' for the trip to Chicago, proved to be an easier task. He is named in the diary, his job as a newspaperman and town of residence are given. His uncommon surname led us to family members in New York and Arizona.

Some notable sights are not mentioned in the diary, such as visits to Machinery Hall, Choral and Music Halls, the Live Stock Pavilion, replica of La Rabida, Dairy Building, and the popular Windmills exhibit. The diarist cannot be blamed; covering 645 acres, the Exposition was just too huge to be seen in two weeks!

Friend Pitts Williams' words are maintained but edited for a few punctuation and spelling errors (Brozel House corrected to Broezel House), minor errors of fact (Ferris Wheel diameter of 260 feet corrected to 250), and minor omissions (South added to Dakota) were filled in to ensure clarity. We have purposely retained possibly offensive words in use in the 1890s such as "Negro," "paleface," and "Indian." To maintain the look of the original diary, Courier New typeface simulating typescript is used along with the symbols Williams added to decorate his title page and text.

Biographies of the diarist, his father, and a trip friend, including their fates as learned from family members and through genealogical, school, and newspaper accounts appear below.

DIARIST: FRIEND PITTS WILLIAMS

The diarist named in the newspaper accounts is Friend Pitts Williams. He was born in Richmond Mills, New York, near Rochester, on December 18, 1875. His parents moved to Olean, New York, in 1884, and he graduated from Olean High School in June of 1893. His August trip to Chicago and the fair may have been a graduation present.

Olean city directories show that he lived with his folks at least until 1894, and left in September of that year for Cornell University in Ithaca, New York. He graduated from Cornell with a degree in civil engineering in 1899. At the university, he was class treasurer and a member of both the Rod and Bob Club and the Beta Theta Pi fraternity.

In 1900 Friend accompanied New York Governor Frank W. Higgins' son Orrin to the Adirondack Mountains when Orrin went there in hopes of restoring his health. Friend stayed with him and reported by letters to the Governor, who was also from Olean; these letters

F. P. Williams

Friend Pitts Williams, Cornell University graduation, 1899. *Cornellian 1898-9,* p 88. (Courtesy of Rare and Manuscript Collections, Cornell University Library)

Friend's obituary portrait in the *Knickerbocker News*, Albany, New York, February 21, 1939. (Courtesy of Albany Public Library)

are held with the Governor's papers and were referenced in a recent thesis: "Frank Wayland Higgins: New York's 'Forgotten Governor.'"

Williams worked for the Pittsburgh, Shawmut and Northern Railroad Company in western New York for five years and became a state engineer in 1904. He married Alma Horton in 1907. She died in 1927 and is interred in the family plot at Mount View Cemetery in Olean. Friend and Alma had two children: Grace, born in 1908, and Emily Louise, born in 1913, both in Albany, New York.

Friend worked on the extensive New York Barge Canal project as an engineer from 1914 to 1921. During World War I he organized a company of volunteer engineers for training. He was appointed to the New York Water Power Commission in 1921. Friend Pitts Williams died in Albany on February 20, 1939, and is buried next to his wife in the family plot at Mount View Cemetery.

Old Olean High School from a period postcard. Friend graduated from this school in 1893. (Courtesy of Olean Historical Society)

FATHER: ALLAN IRVING WILLIAMS

Friend's father and traveling companion was Allan Irving Williams. He was born on January 20, 1846, the son of wagon maker George Wright. Wright died about 1851, and Allan was adopted by Demian D. and Emily Williams, who gave him their surname. His new parents farmed 160 acres in Bennington, Shiawassee County, Michigan, starting in 1852.

Allan joined the Union Army on August 30, 1862, was wounded at the Civil War battle of Gettysburg, and was honorably discharged in 1865. He married Emily Barton in 1869, and six years later they moved to Richmond Mills, New York, as co-owners of a grist mill. Their first son, Friend Pitts, was born there. Allan and Emily had two more sons, Allan B. and Myron P. Williams.

Allan became head bookkeeper for the Acme Oil Company in Olean in 1884. The family lived in at least three homes in Olean, the last one in the 1890s was located at 95 Sullivan. Allan was a pillar of the community, serving on the school board and as city alderman. He became secretary and treasurer for an oil business, the Associated Producers Company, Olean, beginning in 1890. In 1895 he was in the office of cashier for the Exchange Bank in Olean. The president of the bank developed Mount View Cemetery, and Allan Williams procured a family plot in it. After he retired from the bank in 1907, Allan was elected a director—a position he held until his death on October 21, 1929. He is buried at Mount View.

The Williams family was talented and hardworking. The youthful Friend Pitts showed his observational and writing skills in his

The Allan I. Williams residence in Olean, New York. Allan and his son left for Chicago from this home. (Courtesy of Olean Historical Society)

Bank portrait of Allan Williams, Esq. (Courtesy of Olean Historical Society)

perceptive account of the Chicago trip, which was typed apparently on his own initiative, as it was not associated with a school assignment.

TRAVELING COMPANION: WALTER LE GRYS

Walter John Le Grys, pronounced "la-grice," met Friend and Allan on the train to Chicago and thus became their unplanned traveling companion. The three stayed at the same hotel near the Columbian Exposition grounds.

Walter was born on April 28, 1862, probably in Cambridge, New York, where family members still live. He graduated from Cambridge Academy preparatory school and Hobart College in Geneva, New York. He was the city editor for the Troy Press his entire career—1887 to 1908—and was working in this capacity when he traveled to Chicago to report on the Exposition. He was also secretary of the Troy Press Company.

In 1908 Le Grys ran on the Democratic ticket for New York state senator, developed "brain fever," narrowly lost the election, and died on November 8, 1908, in Troy, New York. He was buried from St. Luke's Church in Troy on November 11, 1908.

1908 campaign card printed by the Typographical Union with a portrait of Walter Le Grys. (Courtesy of Kenneth LeGrys)

```
$$$$$                                    $$$$$
$                                            $
$                                            $
```

RECOLLECTIONS OF

THE WORLD'S COLUMBIAN EXPOSITION

—:Chicago   1893:—

Opened May 1st-   Closed Oct. 30th-

Our visit was during the latter half of August.

```
$$$$$                                    $$$$$
$                                            $
$                                            $
```

Recollections of a Trip to the World's Fair

Chicago-1893.

Father and I left Olean, New York (Fig. 1),
at four on the afternoon of August seventeenth, and, arriving in Buffalo (Fig. 2) about
seven, we took supper at the Broezel House
(Fig. 3). We left here about nine for Chicago.
The sleeper we occupied was the "Atlanta."
General Sanford, a lecturer and traveler, told
some of his interesting experiences and
stories during the trip. I didn't sleep very
soundly, but looked out several times at the

Fig. 1. Olean, New York, train station for the Pennsylvania Railroad to Buffalo (above).
(Courtesy of Olean Historical Society)

Fig. 2. Buffalo, New York, train station (right) at 21 Exchange Street after the turn of the century.
(Buffalo Historical Society)

Fig. 3. The Broezel House (below) hotel and well-known city restaurant on Seneca just two short blocks up Wells Street from the train station.
(Buffalo Historical Society)

passing towns and Lake Shore (Fig. 4). We arrived at our destination about eleven o'clock next morning, and soon chose "The Portland" (Fig. 5) as our stopping place. We found very good accommodations here, and it was very convenient; for an entrance to the grounds was directly across the street from it.

Fig. 4. The Lake Shore Railway timetable from Buffalo to Chicago with bird's-eye view of the fairgrounds on the cover. This route followed the scenic Lake Erie shoreline and featured Wagner sleeping cars, which Williams mentions later.

Fig. 5. The Portland Hotel (white arrow) at 288 60th Street in Hyde Park as viewed from the Ferris Wheel on the Midway looking east to Lake Michigan. (Location courtesy of the Chicago Historical Society; today the address is 1441 East 60th Street.)

Walter Le Grys (Fig. 6), a young gentleman we met just as we left the train, stopped at the same Hotel with us. He came from Troy; his business there being with the Troy Press (Fig. 7). He was a fine young fellow, and we enjoyed his company very much.

Fig. 6. Walter Le Grys in the 1890s. (Courtesy of Marilyn LeGrys Decker)

Fig. 7. Bannerhead for the Troy Press. (Courtesy of Troy Public Library)

After dinner, we three set out to see the big show, and merely had to cross the street to gain admittance (Fig. 8), as I said before, but you, of course had to pay an admission fee, which was fifty cents (Fig. 9). Nearly all the afternoon was spent in viewing the grounds and getting our bearings. It is, indeed, a grand sight to the newcomer, and one that does not grow tiresome; for you could sit down at any and all times, and study with great interest the beauty of the

Fig. 8. Entrance to the Columbian Exposition at Stoney Island Avenue and 62nd Street near the Portland Hotel.

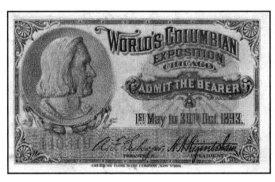

Fig. 9. The Columbus ticket, one of six souvenir general admission ticket designs. Admission was 50¢.

The World's Columbian Exposition was a grand celebration marking the 400th anniversary of Columbus's landing in the New World.

mammoth white palaces. The arrangement of the buildings and planning of the grounds seems to have been done with great care and study; for everything is in harmony with its surroundings. We walked around the buildings awhile, and finally took a trip on the Intramural Railroad (Fig. 10), an electric elevated railroad skirting the grounds.

Fig. 10. The north terminal of the Intramural Railroad at the Fisheries Building as seen from the top of the Government Building. A round trip was 10¢.

The Administration Building (Fig. 11) is very artistic and beautiful. It has an immense dome. A person standing in under it, looking high above at the interior decorations and pictures, is very apt to appreciate its immensity by having his neck strained

Fig. 11. The Administration Building east entrance. The gilded dome of this lofty building was 220 feet in height.

in gazing over its whole surface. Under it, is a facsimile of the Treasury Building (Fig. 12) at Washington made of Columbian half-dollars.

Fig. 12. The replica of the U.S. Treasury Building in Columbian half-dollars flanked by Columbian Guards. It was located under the dome of the Administration Building.

The Western Union Telegraph Co. has a large office in the Building, as have some large Express Companies; and I understand

that the offices of the chief officials of
the Exposition are situated in this building.

We entered Krupp's Pavilion (Fig. 13), where
we found a large display of cannons and large

Fig. 13. The Krupp Building near the lakeshore was sponsored by the famous armament manufacturer of Essen, Germany.

Fig. 14. Krupp Building interior showing the world's largest gun (125 tons) and a shell display. The attendant (arrow) on the carriage stairway is dwarfed by the exhibit.

Fig. 15. The giant rudder and ocean steamer screw exhibit in the Krupp Building.

castings. The largest cannon ever cast was very conspicuous (Fig. 14), and near by was an immense rudder frame (Fig. 15), a screw for an ocean steamer, twenty-two feet high, very large shaftings, and the huge beak of an iron-clad. Several large forgings (castings), eight or ten inches thick, stood next the wall. These are samples of the covering of warships (Fig. 16), but by the impressions made in them by cannon balls, they showed that they were by no means impenetrable to modern warfare. Some balls had merely hollowed out a small cavity; others of more force had made deeper impressions, curled up a rough rim at their entrance, and swelled the thickness of the sheet about their passage; while the most powerful had penetrated entirely through.

Fig. 16. Pierced armor display against the left wall. Krupp Building.

We went aboard the "Santa Maria" (Fig. 17), an exact reproduction of the original chief boat of Columbus. It was a quaint craft indeed. Aboard it, were ancient arms (Fig. 18), an old style ship stove, an old compass, a three-legged kettle labeled "The first casting in America," and many other

Fig. 17. The *Santa Maria* full-sized replica built by Spain, sailed to the Columbian Exposition, and moored at the east end of the Agricultural Building.

Fig. 18. Captain's quarters on the *Santa Maria* replica.

quaint ship implements. Representatives of his other two ships, the "Pinta" and "Nina" (Fig. 19), lay close by, but were not open for the public to go aboard.

Fig. 19. The *Pinta* and *Nina* replicas from Spain. Agricultural Building is in the background.

We inspected the Battleship, "Illinois" (Fig. 20), a little later. This is an exact reproduction of the battleship of the same name in

Fig. 20. The *U.S.S. Illinois* replica exhibit on Lake Michigan at the north end of the fairgrounds.

the U. S. Navy, but is built up from the bottom of the lake with bricks. This we found a very popular place; there being a great stream of persons going off and on all the while. Around on deck, there were guns of various sizes and kinds shielded by massive armor plates (Fig. 21). Down below, many nautical instruments, a model of the bottom of the Atlantic Ocean, implements for raising the large heavy shells to the deck, and very nice cabins fitted up for the superior officers, were some of the interesting sights I remember in this exhibit. There were also cozy cots and hammocks for the sick, while close at hand was a large assortment of medicines. The commissary's room showed the bill-of-fare that the men of our Navy have. Several nice models of other warships were exhibited.

Fig. 21. Guns and armor on the battleship *Illinois* exhibit.

The Viking Ship (Fig. 22), an imitation of
the one which the Norsemen first came to this
country in, was anchored close by the "Illinois."
It wasn't a very large boat, and its means of
propulsion was by oars. A great dragon's head
formed the beak of the boat, and long rows of
round shields lined the sides.

Fig. 22. The Viking Ship replica was sailed from Norway to the Columbian Exposition and
moored east of the Government Building, which is seen in the left background. The prow and
stern figureheads are now held by the Museum of Science and Industry Archives, Chicago.

The West Point Cadets (Fig. 23) arrived in
the afternoon, and made a fine appearance as
they marched across the grounds to their
camping place on the Government Building
Plaza. Their erect forms, straight backs, and
finely fitting clothes made them appear
great. By way of incident I might tell of the
story two of the Cadets played in while here.

Fig. 23. Drill of the smart West Point Cadets bivouaced on the Government Plaza parade grounds near the lakeshore. The battleship *Illinois* exhibit is in the background and an electric lamp standard is prominent in the foreground.

These two — one of them holding the highest position among the cadets at the Academy, and an expected graduate of the next year's class — decided to have a lark and sneak off after taps to have supper up at the Palmer House. They were told on by a guard, and were quartered in a tent all the time they were not on duty while they stayed at the Exposition. Besides, an examination of the case was to be held on their return to West Point to see whether they should be expelled or not.*

In the evening we spent much time in admiring the great electrical display. There is no doubt but that it was done on a scale never before conceived. The display consists

* Although relieved of their duties and demoted, they were not expelled.

Fig. 24. The night illumination of the Court of Honor and Grand Basin. Machinery Hall is on the left, the Administration Building in the center, and the Manufactures Building is in the right foreground.

in illuminating the Court of Honor (indeed it was one), and the Grand Basin with long rows of incandescent lights (Fig. 24). These were in reality about eighteen inches apart, but from the ground they, of course, didn't seem more than half that space. These line the cornices of all the Buildings bordering the Court: this is to include the beautiful lighted Peristyle (Fig. 25). Long lines of lights, also, extended around the Grand Basin, about four feet from the water. The Administration Building (Fig. 26) was especially illuminated, and especially beautiful. The large dome was brilliantly illuminated by rows of lights lining its ridges, and at the balconies on each of its four sides were large gas jets.

This could be seen a long ways off, and formed a fitting crown for the Great Show.

Fig. 25. The illuminated Peristyle and Grand Basin looking east toward Lake Michigan from the Administration Building. MacMonnies Fountain is in the foreground.

Fig. 26. The illuminated Administration Building.

The Electrical Fountains (Fig. 27) played between eight and nine. There are two of these: one on the right, the other on the left, in front of the Administration Building, and in the Grand Basin. The beautiful MacMonnies Fountain (Fig. 28) with its ever continuous sprays of water is situated between the two. The Electric Fountains throw jets of water and spray of various colors and combinations of colors high up in the air. By varying the manner in which the water was thrown up, sheaves of wheat were imitated in a very natural manner. The

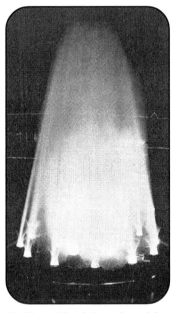

Fig. 27. An Electric Fountain at night. Large color wheels under each lamp of the fountain were used to change the display.

Fig. 28. MacMonnies Fountain illuminated by the great search light on Manufactures.

Fig. 29. The illuminated
Electrical Building, 340 feet
wide by 700 feet.

Fig. 30. One of the many electric
lamp and hardware displays.

Fig. 31. The Westinghouse
illuminated Columbus board in
the Electrical Building. The
American Bell Telephone
pavilion is in the foreground.

Electrical Building (Fig. 29) was visited for a short time in the evening. The interior is brilliantly illuminated, making it an excellent place to come in the evening, and also because the illumination was the chief thing to see. Electric lamps (Fig. 30) in a great variety of sizes, shapes, colors, and arranged in all sorts of ways, were present on all sides. A picture of Columbus outlined by lights (Fig. 31), adorned a large space on one of the walls. A tall column (Fig. 32) in the center of the building was a pleasing sight, and showed much skill and ingenuity in arranging lights. Around its sides curved lines of light of many colors oscillated to and fro, and in many ways, kept time with the orchestra which played in the gallery.

Fig. 32. The grand Edison tower illuminated at night.

Fig. 33. The Western Electric illuminated tower with spiral bulbs and lighted zigzag arms.

A tower (Fig. 33) up which a ball of light went at intervals and branched off on lightning shaped arms 'til it reached a revolving ball, which changed colors as it revolved, was another freak sight. A boot-blacking machine, a pocket thief detective, and other novel devices showed uses that electricity had been put to by some ingenious minds. An automatic machine was so construc-ted, that a long pointer would go over letters made of incandescent lamps, light them up, and then go back over them again and put all out. A darkened room, where artificial lightning (Fig. 34)

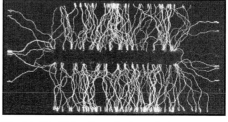

Fig. 34. The high voltage display, Nikola Tesla exhibit.

was produced, attracted considerable attention
by the frequent passages of electricity from
one pole to the other.

- : - : - : - : - : -

Fig. 35. The Horticultural Building of Venetian renaissance style had a thousand-foot
frontage and a glass dome 114 feet in height. The main entrance is shown.

Saturday, Aug. 19. Father and I went
first to the Horticultural Building (Fig. 35).
In a small outside building, we found a nice
display of gloxinias (Fig. 36). Under the immense
dome of the Main
Building was a
conical shaped
mass of foliaged
plants, consist-
ing of tropical
ferns, palms and
many other varie-
ties. Under this

Fig. 36. Gloxinia display in the New York outdoor
section of the Horticultural Building.

Fig. 37. Crystal Cave exhibit from South Dakota was located under the central dome of the Horticultural Building. Admission was free.

Fig. 38. Giant tree ferns in the Australian exhibit.

Fig. 39. Mexican cactus garden.

Fig. 40. German Rhine wine exhibit. Horticultural Building, south court.

mass was a Crystal Cave (Fig. 37), lined throughout with crystal formations taken from a cave in South Dakota. Some noticeable things in this building were the immense tree ferns (Fig. 38), orchids growing naturally on a tree trunk, tall large cactus (Fig. 39), begonias, a huge lawn mower, German wine exhibit (Fig. 40), paintings of the Rhine Valley, California orange tower (Fig. 41), containing 13,873 oranges, cans of large nice peaches, pears, plums, and grapes. There was a large number of plates of fresh fruits and vegetables; of apples in particular. In the court was an orange grove; I noticed a few oranges on the trees.

Fig. 41. The California Orange Tower stood 35 feet in height and was surmounted by an eagle with outstretched wings. The almost 14,000 oranges were renewed every three to four weeks during the Fair, showing that California could supply citrus to the Exposition from May through October. The exhibit was in an area known as the "South Rear Curtain" of the Horticultural Building.

Next was the Transportation Building (Fig. 42). This, unlike the other buildings, had its decorations on the outside done in various shades of red, and was very pretty in contrast with the others. The Main Entrance which had a greenish silvery appearance was magnificent (Fig. 43). We first happened on some fine models of warships; one of which was the ill-fated "Victoria" Battleship (Fig. 44), which, it will be remembered, was lost in a collision

Fig. 42. Transportation Building. Designed by Louis Sullivan and David Adler. The only major building that was not painted white was 960 feet long and fronted the central Lagoon.

Fig. 43. Golden Door, the famous main entrance to the Transportation Building.

Fig. 44. Model of the ill-fated *Victoria* battleship with torpedo skirt.

with another ironclad in the Mediterranean
Sea. It sunk in thirteen minutes with about
four hundred lives aboard. The model, about
fifteen feet long, was a nice piece of
workmanship. What particularly attracted my
attention about it was the woven steel ringed
shield held out from its sides to protect it
from torpedoes. The Mexican National R. R. had
an interesting exhibit. It consisted mainly
of the equipments of the Mexican horsemen:
especially, some finely embroidered saddles.
Close by, was an automatic check hook. A
fancy northern-style sleigh made by a large
N. Y. firm, attracted much attention. A relief
map of Pullman, Ill. (Fig. 45), a miniature
Temple of Edfou, a copper plate from which a
large map of the U. S. could be printed were
exhibited. Foreign locomotives of different
patterns from ours, and a section of a large
ocean steamer (Fig. 46) occupied considerable

Fig. 45. An 80-foot model of Pullman, Illinois, as exhibited in the Transportation Building.

Fig. 46. American Line steamship exhibit was provided by the International Navigation Company. The section exhibited was more than 70 feet long and 35 feet wide, or 1/7 the entire length of the ship then under construction by William Cramp and Sons, Philadelphia. The floor of the Transportation Building represented the water line. The promenade deck was 25 feet above the floor and the top of the funnel an additional 53 feet.

space. The first cabins and dining room (Fig. 47) in the section were furnished beautifully. Bethlehem Iron Co.'s steam hammer (Fig. 48) was an immense affair— a whole circus parade, you know, could go under the hammer and never touch.

Fig. 47. Steamship dining room constructed from white mahogony had light green panelings.

Fig. 48. One man under the Bethlehem Iron Company's massive hammer exhibit. The imposing structure, 90 feet high with a span of 40 feet, was a reproduction of the world's largest steam forging hammer. The original mechanism weighed more than 2000 tons; the replica was of wood and staff.

Some large cannons were displayed here also; a twelve inch was among them. The different styles of Turkish carriers were shown, and the Sedan chair (Fig. 49). Naphtha launches (Fig. 50) and sailboats were nearby in great variety. There were some beauties among them.

Fig. 49. Turkish sedan chair in the Transportation Building. These chairs were also a popular mode of transportation on the Midway.

Fig. 50. Naphtha Launch as illustrated on the Morris Heights, New York, Gas Engine and Power Company's die-cut ad. These launches were not allowed to ply the lagoons; only non-vapor-emitting craft were permitted there by fairground rules.

The Fisheries Building (Fig. 51) was next looked into. This time, only the main part was visited. A number of seines (Fig. 52), nets, and fish dams to catch fish in, were the first things to meet our gaze. A whale's skeleton (Fig. 53) was exhibited, and an arch made of its jaws (Fig. 54), so one could say

Fig. 51. Fisheries Building. The structure consisted of the large main building (shown here) and a circular "Angling Pavilion" on either side, which held fresh and seawater aquariums. The length of the building, including the two pavilions, was 1100 feet.

Fig. 52. Seines over the Canadian exhibit. Fisheries Building.

Fig. 53. Fisheries Building. Whale skeleton at the Washington State exhibit.

that he had walked through a whale's jaws, if he wished to say so. Cans of fish, principally salmon were on all sides, and there were several nicely mounted fish. The sturgeon, saw-fish, salmon, and some seals were noticeable among them. In the Japanese section,

Fig. 54. Whale jawbone entrance to Washington State exhibit in Fisheries.

we found seaweed (Fig. 55) prepared as a food; it is of a light flaky texture.

After a little rest, two of the foreign buildings were visited. In the India Building (Fig. 56), there was a great deal of expensive work in silver, copper and brass. Nearly, if not all the work in this

Fig. 55. Japanese seaweed bales in Fisheries.

line, as well as in all their other exhibits was done by hand. A great deal of sandalwood

Fig. 56. The ornamented India Building was erected by the India Tea Company of Calcutta.

Fig. 57. Interior of the India Building containing rich exhibits of silks, ivory, carvings, lacquer work, inlays of gold and silver, bronze castings, embroideries, and carpets.

carving was exhibited, and folding screens of carved ebony inlaid with ivory were very handsome and costly too. Rugs in quite a variety, as well as other dry goods, were displayed (Fig. 57). The Swedish

Fig. 58. The Swedish Building design was based on churches and gentlemen's houses of the 16th and 17th centuries.

Building (Fig. 58) was very interesting, also. Quite a gymnasium was fitted up here, and the walls were lined with pictures of the various movements in physical culture. This showed that these people were, likely, looking toward this line of pastime. Snow shoes, skates, saws—the largest band saw in the world—, axes, a variety of valuable furs, and a paper roll ten feet wide, I remember seeing.

- : - : - : - : - : -

Sunday, Aug. 20. We found most of the State Buildings closed today. There were two, however, where visitors were admitted. The Michigan Building (Fig. 59) was mainly intended for the comfort of its visitors; there being but few exhibits in it. Large nice mantels and two nice grand pianos were the interior furnishings that particularly caught my eye.

Fig. 59. The Michigan Building with ground dimensions of 140 by 100 feet was three stories plus an observatory.

Fig. 60. The Washington State Building was constructed from native wood and stone. Its monumental flagstaff (at left in photo), hewn from a single tree, was 208 feet in height.

Fig. 61. Realistic farm scene in the Washington State Building.

One of the pianos was finished off in light, and, I would say, in old style. The Washington Building (Fig. 60), on the other hand, contained mostly exhibits. One section contained a number of specimens of coal and the ores of its native metals. The central division was occupied by its cereal products. A view of a farm laid out in relief was very nicely done (Fig. 61). The house, barn, men, and horses working in the grain were very natural. Fine pieces of taxidermy varied the display. A deer, elk, pelican, white and black bears, seal, cougar, and the skeleton of a great mastodon were noticeable. Another department was devoted to school work, physical culture, embroidery, and needlework.

Fig. 62. The Fine Arts Building. Designed by C. B. Atwood in the Grecian-Ionic style. The main building (pictured) was 500 feet wide with 125-foot high central dome. The south entrance (at left in photo) fronted the North Pond. After the fair the building was the Field Columbian Museum; since 1933 it has been the Museum of Science and Industry.

The Fine Arts Building was next visited (Fig. 62). The large interior rooms of courts were occupied by statuary, and along the sides of the courts were the rooms containing the paintings. The finely carved, snowy white, statuary marble was very beautiful. The two

Fig. 63. Entrance to the Japanese section in the Fine Arts Building.

Fig. 64. Japanese fine art vases. Nine-foot cloisonne vases on either side of a ceramic incense burner. The vase with rooster design described by Williams is on the right.

large vases in the Japanese section (Fig. 63)
must have attracted everybody's attention.
The first process in their manufacture is the
hammering of a metal (I think copper or
silver) in the shape of the vase (Fig. 64).
Then, it is enameled with some substance, and
pictures—one had a rooster on it—are wrought
upon them. The last process is in finely
polishing it. Some of the pictures in the
United States section impressed me most, but
by the following list of remembrances, most
of the different nations are represented.

Forging the Anchor	Forbes	G. B.
The Hunt Ball (Fig. 65)	Stewart	U. S.

Fig. 65. "The Hunt Ball" by Jules L. Stewart, Paris, France.

Christmas Bells (Fig. 66)	Blashfield	" "
Rent Day	Kappes	" "
Nantucket School of Philosophy	E. Johnson	" "

Fig. 66. "Christmas Bells" by Edwin H. Blashfield, New York, New York.

Fig. 67. "Alice" by William M. Chase, New York, New York.

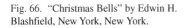

Alice (Fig. 67)	W. M. Chase	" "
Peace	W. L. Dean	U. S.
Breaking Home Ties	Hovendon	U. S.
The Empty Saddle (Fig. 68)	Waller	G. B.
Girl With Horse	Tarbell	U. S.
In the Omnibus	Zorn	Sweden
Scouts in Flight	Guiguard	France
Contesting Ownership of the Apple of Contentment	Hartman	Germany
Reading Homer	Alma Tadema	"
Fisherman	Gilbert	France
Young Girl Chasing Butterfly	Russel	France
The Flagellants	Marr	U. S.
Passing the Ring	Bartholomew	France
Carnot at Wattignies	DeTours	France
Miners on a Strike	Touche	"
On the Yacht Namouna, Venice, 1890.	Jules Stewart	U. S.
Baptism	Stewart	U. S.
Bringing Home The Bride	Hovendon	U. S.

Fig. 68. "The Empty Saddle" by S.E. Waller, London, Great Britain.

Fig. 69. "A Card Trick" by J.G. Brown, New York, New York.

A Card Trick (Newsboys) (Fig. 69)	J.G. Brown	" "
Embarkation of Columbus by Order of Boadilla	Menocal	Spain
A Strike in Viscaya	Cutanda	"
First Homage Paid to Columbus (Landing)	Garneto	"
Under the Awning	Bernundo	Spain
A Rooster with Long Tail on Plum Tree Hen with Chickens Below	Otaka	Japan
Surprised	Boks	Holland
Statuary		Italy
Romeo & Juliet	Makovsky	Russia
Several Pictures of Columbus and his Voyage	Aivazovosky	"
George Washington (equestrian)	Huber	Austria
The Pages	Charlemont	"
The Five Senses	Markart	"
Emperor William II	Winner	Germany
The Harvest Repast	Hensler	Germany
Rolling Mill	Bordes	France
Melody	Holman	U. S.
Sea Urchins	Sewell	U. S.

Fig. 70. "Singing School in a Common School in Paris" by Auguste Trupheme, Paris, France.

Admiral Farragut	Weir	U. S.
The Rod (Fisherman)	Gilber	France
The Royal Danish Family	Tuxen	Denmark
Sappho	Spindon	Italy
The Lovers	Binet	France
Victory of Faith	Hare	G. B.
Pickwick Club	Green	" "
Singing School in a Common School in Paris (Fig. 70)	Trupheme	France
At the Capstan	Couturier	France
In the Orchard	Tarbell	U. S.
Emigrants Embarking at Antwerp	Farasyn	Belgium
My Studio-Cut Obliquely by the Author on Account of Jealousy	Kahler	Germany
Foxes	Liljefors	Sweden
Ball	Zorn	Sweden
The Sudden Attack	Brandt	Germany
The Dice Throwers	Hamza	Austria
Fisherman Returning Home	Ancher	Denmark
Goodbye	Braendekilde	Denmark
Interior of a Stable	Hslund	"
Oliver Twist Walks to London	Hunt	G. B.

Fig. 71. The Mines Building with five and a half acres of floor space was of early Italian renaissance design. The arched entrance was fifty-six feet high.

After dinner, we visited the gallery in the Mines Building (Fig. 71). The Standard Oil Company's exhibit (Figs. 72 & 73) was quite interesting, as it brings one back to a home industry. A sectional view showed the oil operations, and the character of the soil throughout the oil territory including Olean. A nice exhibit of oils, vaseline, also, pictures of refineries, fine piano lamps, a miniature oil refinery were the chief things in this display. The tile floor showed that extra precautions had been taken about this exhibit. Some time was spent looking over Ward's Natural History exhibit, which seemed to be endless in extent; there being case after case of minerals. Samples of marble, beryl, topaz, tourmaline, agate, and the more precious gems were some that I noticed by

Fig. 72. Standard Oil Pavilion facade. Second floor gallery, Mines Building.

Fig. 73. Inside the Standard Oil exhibit in the Mines Building.

looking at the labels. There were several
interesting coins in the exhibit of Kunz of
New York. There was a Swedish piece, (1737),
a sheet of copper about a 1/4 of an inch thick

and ten inches square, whose par value was
four dollars; Egyptian coins of the times of
Cleopatra, Siamese porcelain coins, a Chinese
coin, perhaps, 2 and 1/2 inches in diameter
with a hole in the center, coin B. C. 60, 388
octagonal gold dollars of the U. S. coinage 1853,
and ancient bullet-shaped coins. An exhibit
showed different shades of gold. A number of
articles made of aluminum, especially cooking
utensils, occupied another section.

- : - : - : - : - : -

Fig. 74. The Turkish Building. Imitation of the Hunkhar Casque of Sultan Ahmed III,
Constantinople. The structure was 80 x 100 feet, surmounted by a small central dome.

Monday, Aug. 21. The Turkish Building
(Fig. 74) was first visited to-day. These
people exhibited fabrics, rugs, enamel work,
and articles with inlaid ivory. Brazil had a

Fig. 75. The popular coffee garden outdoors at the Brazil Building. Coffee was free of charge.

Fig. 76. The Brazil Building in the form of a Greek cross was of French
renaissance architectural design. Height to the top of the cupola was 150 feet.

very large assortment of coffees (Fig. 75) in
her building (Fig. 76). The Illinois Building
(Fig. 77), the largest state building on the
grounds, was largely devoted to exhibits.

Fig. 77. Facing the Lagoon, the Illinois Building, largest of the state buildings, was 450 feet wide. Surmounting the building was a dome rising 235 feet. The building was constructed of native Illinois materials and finished with an exterior coating of white staff.

Fig. 78. The twelve-inch-deep fish pond of filtered lake water with waterfall and brook was located inside the Illinois Building. It was an exhibit of the Illinois State Fish Commission.

Fig. 79. This enormous Illinois farm scene hand-crafted of grains and grasses by Illinois school girls was 24 x 32 feet. The intricately designed four-foot frame was constructed of yellow corn.

Birds and animals mounted, birds' eggs and dissected small animals were noticeable. A little artificial brook with fish (Fig. 78) in it furnished variety to the scene. Exhibits of fruits, vegetables, a large farm scene (Fig. 79) made of corn of different shades, and Indian relics occupied considerable time in looking over.

The Florida Building (Fig. 80) was built in imitation of Fort Marion, St. Augustine's historic Fort. Souvenirs (Fig. 81) were principally sold here. Arizona and New Mexico had nothing particularly interesting in their building (Figs. 82 & 83).

Fig. 80. The Florida Building was a miniature of Fort Marion, St. Augustine, Florida. It was one-fifth the size of the original; including the moat, the site was 155 feet square. The frame was of pine covered with plaster and coquina shells, in imitation of the original. Palm tree landscaping was featured, as were gardens planted in the dry moat.

Fig. 81. Curios in the Florida State Building gift shop.

Fig. 82. The Joint Territorial Building—New Mexico, Arizona, and Oklahoma. The building had a ninety-foot frontage and a cactus garden exhibit on the roof.

Fig. 83. The New Mexico Pecos River Valley display in the Joint Territorial Building.

The Pennsylvania Building was a finely furnished building (Fig. 84). The old historic Liberty Bell (Fig. 85) made this an attractive visiting place.

The New York Building (Fig. 86) came next, and seemed best of all. It looked very neat from the outside, and its interior was furnished very richly. The floors were mosaic, and were covered with large fine rugs.

Fig. 84. The Pennsylvania State Building was an exact reproduction of old Independence Hall. The 110 x 166 foot building had 800 electric lamps.

Fig. 85. The Liberty Bell on display in the Pennsylvania State Building.

There were no industrial exhibits, but some of the furniture had historic interest attached

Fig. 86. The New York State Building, designed as an Italian renaissance villa, was finished in staff imitating marble, like the main Exposition buildings. It was illuminated by 2000 "electric jets," and its three stories were crowned with a roof promenade and summer garden.

Fig. 87. New York State Building entrance hall foyer looking toward the reading room wing in the distance.

to it; besides this there were other relics of the past. The furniture was a deep black in color, and decorated with much carving. A room was devoted to the newspapers of the State (Fig. 87), and a place to write letters. Elevators took people to the roof, but I didn't go up. I wrote my name on the big book for the visitors to register upon. A large painting of Chauncey M. Depew (Fig. 88) hung over one of the mantels.

Fig. 88. Portrait of Chauncey M. Depew over the mantel in the New York State Building.

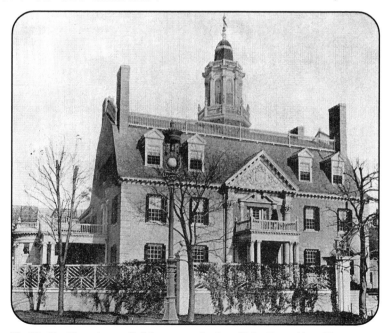

Fig. 89. The Massachusetts Building, a reproduction of John Hancock's residence.

The Massachusetts Building (Fig. 89) was built in the likeness of the typical old style New England dwellings. Many old relics were exhibited here, also. Old chairs, a pine tree shilling, old bills, calendars, & Scarlet Letter Law, the foundation of the famous "Scarlet Letter" by Hawthorne, were interesting (Fig. 90).

Fig. 90. Essex Institute room of historical documents. Massachusetts Building.

Vermont's (Fig. 91) was a small structure, where a little marble was all to be seen. Maine's building (Fig. 92) was next visited.

Fig. 91. The Vermont State Building of Pompeiian style.

Fig. 92. The Maine State Building. An octagonal structure with a ground area of 65 feet square, the highest point was 86 feet. The first floor was constructed of Maine granite and the overhanging second floor of Maine wood and staff.

After the fair, the Maine Building was removed from Chicago and recon-structed in Poland Spring, Maine. It now is home to the Maine Historical Society.

Fig. 93. The Ceylon Building (above) was 162 feet in length and styled after the richly orna-mented ancient Singhalese temples.

Fig. 94. Tusks and carved ivory in the Ceylon Building. The wall of the central octa-gonal hall is to the left in this photo.

Ceylon's Building (Fig. 93) had chiefly tea, ivory work (Fig. 94), and mummies.

The Germans (Fig. 95) made a specialty of ecclesiastical work (Fig. 96) in their Building. A large clock with performing figures was quite a piece of mechanism, but I didn't see it in operation. A large assortment of German books was here too (Fig. 97).

Fig. 95. The German Building (above) was Gothic German renaissance design and 130 feet long facing Lake Michigan. The Byzantine-style bell tower was 105 feet in height.

Fig. 96. The interior of the 39-foot wide chapel (left) that was appended to the German Building.

Fig. 97. Book and literature exhibits in the main room of the German Building.

Fig. 98. The Spain Building, modeled after the Casa Lonja of Valencia, fronted the lake and was 84½ feet wide.

Fig. 99. Interior of the Spain Building consisted of fifteen vaulted areas supported by pillars. A major display was 12,000 bottles of choice wine.

Spain's was a cold disinteresting building (Figs. 98 & 99).

We now went over to finish the annex of the Transportation Building. We went through the Pullman Palace Train of five cars (Fig. 100). They were princely indeed. The finishing in mahogany, and it was very richly carved and polished. Onyx wash basins, a bathroom, barbershop, dining car (Fig. 101), the table being set with silver and fine linen, and a section car were some of the elegant features about the train. An old-time train of the Boston and Providence R. R. (Fig. 102) was near by, and made quite a contrast with the modern Pullman or Wagner. A four-

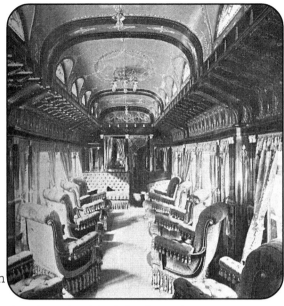

Fig. 100.   Interior of the plush Pullman palace car. Transportation Building Annex.

Fig. 101.   Tables set in crystal and silver in the Pullman dining car.

Fig. 102. The Boston and Providence Railroad engine and coal tender. Transportation Building.

wheeled German car looked odd enough. One of
their coaches was here also. Two large ocean
buoys gave many of the inlanders a surprise,
I imagine. We went through the Empire State
Express Train, which was composed of very long
nicely furnished cars. The engine that draws
it, 999, is a monster (Fig. 103). The boiler
setting up quite high from the tracks was a
noticeable feature. It has made a mile in 32

Fig. 103. Engine Number 999 of New York's Empire State Express. The land-speed record
holder in 1893 now is an exhibit of the Museum of Science and Industry, Chicago.

Fig. 104. English coach cars with side doors. Transportation Building exhibits.

seconds. Many of the drive wheels of the
engines around were much taller than your
head. The B.&O. models of the earliest to
the latest patterns of engines told the
interested person the history of railroad
science. One model exhibited the laughable
idea of moving a train by a pusher out
behind. The engine was designed to follow the
train and in some way the piston rod was made
to shove a stick out behind which pushed the
train along. The English coaches (Fig. 104) were
in sections: the first, second, and third class.
The seats in the cars were crosswise and the
doors at the side, so that to get into them you
had to climb a ladder. One of the British
engines had the water scoop attachment. This
scoops the water from a trough between the
rails, while the train is in motion. The
Gallery contained a large assortment of

Fig. 105. Bicycle exhibit had rotating wheels and mannequin riders. Transportation Building.

bicycles; some with men and women models (Fig. 105) on them and in motion. In several places wheels were in motion to show the small resistance of ball bearings. The old style "Walk" bicycle was exhibited & nearby were several styles of folding boats (Fig. 106).

Fig. 106. Folding boats. Michigan exhibit in the Transportation Building.

Fig. 107. Terminal Railway Station depot, 200 feet long and of Roman-Corinthian style architecture, faced the Administration Building. Thirty-five tracks fed into it.

We visited the depot of the grounds (Fig. 107). It was constructed to show the modern means of handling the public at a railroad station. It was not a success, because very few of the railroads deliver their passengers there. At a desk in the depot information could be obtained in all languages. Along the walls in the main court of the structure, a number of clocks (Fig. 108) tell the time in the principal places of the world.

Fig. 108. Twenty-four clocks, each five feet in diameter, were located above the main Station archways.

The electrical display and fountains
were seen in the evening. We took a trip on
the Movable Sidewalk (Fig. 109) at night too.
This is a constantly moving platform with seats
on it extending far out into the lake on a pier.
This was a beautiful ride this summer evening,
and the grounds lighted by the innumerable
lights, indeed, appeared as a "Magic City."

-:-:-:-:-:-

Fig. 109. Movable Sidewalk and Long Pier on Lake Michigan. Five cents for a one-way ride.

Tuesday, Aug. 22. The Mines Building
(Fig. 110) was the first attraction this morning.
A chunk of cannel coal (Fig. 111) weighing twelve
tons, was a prominent exhibit. An enterprising
salt firm had modeled a woman in salt (Fig. 112)
and titled it "Lot's wife turned to salt."
There was a fine inlaid table, which, I think, a

card explained as being made by a Mexican, who had contributed it to show his heartfelt thanks to the Americans who had shown him the art. It showed that much time and labor had been spent upon it. In one of the State booths, a silver brick looked very attractive, someway. Then, in another place there was a gold nugget valued at $2600. The silver brick and other valuables were

Fig. 110. Front entrance to the Mines Building.

Fig. 111. British exhibit. Twelve tons of cannel coal on display in the Mines Building.

stolen during the latter part of the Exposition. Some sections of trees in petrified form imitated nature very closely indeed. They varied much in diameter; some being one, while others were as much as three feet, and the cross sections were polished as smooth as agate. I was much surprised at the huge chunks of copper exhibited. They were from Michigan mines

Fig. 112. "Lot's Wife." A pillar of salt in the form of a woman. Louisiana display in the Mines Building.

Fig. 113. Michigan exhibit entrance. Mines Building.

(Fig. 113), and in their natural state except for being chipped off to show the pure copper of which they were composed. The large irregular chunks (Fig. 114) weighed six and eight thousand pounds.

Fig. 114. Copper "chunk" displayed in the Michigan exhibit. Mines Building.

As might be expected the Ada Rehan statue of silver in the Montana Section was well gazed at (Fig. 115). The figure was a little larger than life size, and rested on a gold base whose value was more than the statue. Several gold nuggets were in a case nearby.

Fig. 115. Ada Rehan was the model for the "Statue of Justice," a silver sculpture that stood eight feet tall and was cast from native ore. Montana exhibit. Mines Building.

Fig. 116. The Agricultural Building, 800 feet long and of classic renaissance architecture, faced the Grand Basin near Lake Michigan. The height of the glass-domed rotunda was 130 feet.

The Agricultural Building (Fig. 116) was next visited. The Cuban Section (Fig. 117) was very aromatic with the odor of a large display of fine tobacco and cigars. A fine Swift car of

Fig. 117. Cigars displayed in elaborate humidors. Cuban Section of the Agricultural Building.

Fig. 118. Swift Refrigerator R.R. car with hanging sides of beef. Agricultural Building.

beef (Fig. 118) showed
the products of the
land devoted to graz-
ing. Artistic designs
made with the differ-
ent shades of corn
(Fig. 119) were
numerous here. Agri-
cultural implements
(Fig. 120) of every
description occupied
a large section, but
we did not spend any
time in it. A very

Fig. 119. Iowa corn exhibit. Agricultural Building.

Fig. 120. Massey Harris Canadian implement exhibit in the Agricultural Building.

long-tailed fowl in one booth was an odd exhibit. A cheese weighing 22000 lbs., the shape of an ordinary cheese, exhibited on a large strong wagon, attracted one's attention to the Canadian exhibit (Fig. 121). In the Gallery, pickles, catsups, cocoa, &

Fig. 121. The Mammoth Cheese exhibit from Canada. Agricultural Building.

Fig. 122. The H.J. Heinz Company's pickle and catsup display. Agricultural Building Gallery. Inset (right) shows the Heinz exhibit gilt die-cut coupon in the shape of a watch charm. Heinz was founded in 1869. Actual size.

cereals were exhibited (Fig. 122) and the public was invited to sample them, but we didn't embrace the opportunity. Quite a novel fake was at a booth exhibiting sardines. A young lady in attendance would offer the visitor an imitation of an opened can of sardines and handed a fork to take them out with. But that person would find them very hard to remove from the can, and very unwholesome.

-:-:-:-:-:-

Fig. 123. Intramural Railroad at the south end of Jackson Park. The G.E. powerhouse for the Intramural was at the very south end of the fairgrounds. Windmills exhibit is in background.

Wednesday, Aug. 23. We went down to the southern part of the grounds the first thing this morning on the Intramural (Fig. 123). The Oil Well

Fig. 124. Dereks of the Oil Well Supply Company exhibit.

Supply Co. (Fig. 124) had quite an extensive exhibit in their line of business. The Indian School I found very interesting (Fig. 125). The School was not in session when I visited it, but a few neatly appearing boys and girls were present and

Fig. 125. Indian School. A two-story frame building 124 feet wide.

showed the character of the pupils. Handwriting
and drawings by the pupils were on exhibition.
They were splendid, and would make many a
paleface blush at their neatness. The writing
was surprisingly well done. Crocheting, typeset-
ting, needle work, shoe making and tailoring
showed what industries have been introduced
among this race of people. I should have said
that Indians were to work here in these different occupations. A lumber wagon built in a good
substantial manner, and painted, was the work
of an Indian boy of seventeen.

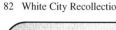

Fig. 126. Part of the 575-foot-long Leather and Shoe Trades Building. Erected in 4 months.

The Shoe and Leather Building (Fig. 126) had its interesting features along with the rest. Shoes of the different countries of the

Fig. 127. Inside the Leather and Shoe Trades Building were many showcases for shoes. The entire second floor was devoted to machinery, including machines for the model shoe factory, which manufactured more than 1000 pairs of shoes a day during the Exposition.

Fig. 128. Elephant hide displayed in the Leather and Shoe Trades Building.

world were exhibited in cases along the wall. Large exhibits of common shoes and different kinds of leather were nice (Fig. 127). A whole alligator's hide and an elephant's hide (Fig. 128), which it took two years to tan, furnished oddity to the display. In the Gallery the different stages of shoe making were shown by different machines in motion.

The Forestry Building (Fig. 129) stands a little beyond this. It does not contain a nail or iron of any kind about it, being built entirely of wood put together with wooden pegs. It must have been quite a feat for the modern carpenters, for the building is quite a large structure. A large section

Fig. 129. The Forestry Building, 500 x 200 feet, was built of wood and had a colonnade of tree trunks, one from every state and each tagged with an identifying plaque.

of a rosewood first attracted my attention, and showed the great beauty of that kind of wood. In several sec-tions, there were rows of polished plank consisting mostly of mahogany and

Fig. 130. Brazil woods finshed with Murphy varnish.

rosewood, but there were many other beautiful woods exhibited; many of which I had never seen before. By tags on the different woods, the Murphy varnish was the principal varnish used in polishing the woods (Fig. 130). A cork pavilion contained many things made of that material. A noticeable article was a cork bath mat which seemed as tho' it might answer its purpose very nicely. The largest plank (Fig. 131) supposed to exist was in one end of the building, and just outside was a large mahogany log (Fig. 132). The Anthropological Building (Fig. 133) was surprisingly interesting. Playing cards and games of

Fig. 131. The world's largest redwood plank, 1500 years old, 16½ feet wide, 13 feet long, was cut in California in June 1890. Displayed by Berry Brothers, varnish manufacturers.

Fig. 132. Mexican mahogany log. Forestry Building veranda.

different countries occupied long rows of cases. Some of the cards (I think the Chinese) were about as long as ours, but only 1/3 as wide, and had characters written up and down

Fig. 133. The Anthropological Building, 415 x 255 feet, was occupied by the Department of Ethnology, which included anthropology and archeology.

upon them. Indian relics by the acre were here, there being case after case of neatly arranged arrowheads (Fig. 134). Skulls, pottery, kettles, pipes, beads, tools, hoes, scalping knives, tomahawks, and graves, just as they were dug up, were here in great variety (Fig. 135). These graves contained the bodies, which were all wrapped up and bound with cord. Some of them had been opened and showed the occupant had been placed in a sitting posture with its legs doubled up against its breast.

The Cliff Dwellers (Fig. 136) is the title of a reproduction of the homes of these ancient inhabitants of Colorado. By this exhibition one can see how their homes were perched on some almost inaccessible cliff. The reproduction was much smaller than the original. Attendants were present to explain different things, making it much more interesting. The relics of the people were exhibited in another chamber.

Fig. 134. Cases of Indian artifacts and implements, Anthropological Building.

Fig. 135. Indian gravesite exhibit from Ancon, Peru, (right) showing skulls on a shelf and unwrapped and seated mummies. Anthropological Building.

Fig. 136. Cliff Dwellers exhibit (left), a reproduction of Colorado's Battle Rock Mountain. Inside (inset above) were caverns containing mummies and utensils found on the original site.

Fig. 137. The whaling bark *Progress* was located in the South Pond. Admission 25¢.

The Whaling Bark "Progress" (Fig. 137) was of little interest compared with innumerable things within a stone's throw, and besides, they were free. Harpoons, whale's jaws, the place for trying out oil, a corset of a Fijian woman, whale bone, log books of the ship, were some of the most interesting things, if you choose to call them so. Going farther northward to the Manufactures Building (Fig. 138), some time was spent among the pianos of different exhibitors. The collection of old pianos was very interesting to me. I never thought of there being such old instruments in existence, or rather had ever existed. Some had only three octaves on their keyboards

Fig. 138. Manufactures Building, the world's largest building under a roof, covered 32 acres with dimensions of 1687 x 787 feet. The building was provided with 10,000 electric lights. Corinthian style architecture.

(Fig. 139). I noticed one, where the color of the keys (Fig. 140) was just the opposite of those

of the present day. Most of them were built in the old square style, were much smaller in size and simpler. A man in charge played on the different ones in turn, but the music was rather tin-panny. They dated back to the seventeenth

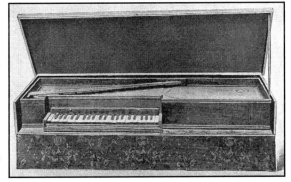

Fig. 139. M. Steinert exhibit, spinet piano of 3½ octaves.

Fig. 140. M. Steinert exhibit, black-key clavichord.

century and thereabouts. Several large displays of modern makes were all that could be asked for in the way of neatness and beauty. The extra long grand pianos (Fig. 141) were the first I had ever seen. Some were finished in white and gold, but most were finished in the natural wood. Chinese ware and vases formed a very costly display. A Chinese vase embossed with gold and about five feet high was valued at $40,000. A beautifully fitted up bathroom pleased me very much. The

Fig. 141. Grand pianos. Hardman exhibit, New York.

floor was of tile; the tub was of the porcelain order, and had a shower & bath attachment; a nice onyx wash stand completed the affair. The Garland Stove Co. made their exhibit prominent by an immense stove raised quite high from the floor (Fig. 142). Similarly, an immense lock marked one of that kind of firm's goods. A long cable wound around a huge reel (Fig. 143)

Fig. 142. Mammoth "Garland" exhibit (right) by the Michigan Stove Company was 25 feet in height, 30 feet long and 20 feet wide.

Fig. 143. J. A. Roebling's Sons Company wire and cable exhibit (below). There were 36,859 feet of cable on the 10-foot diameter reel.

was "tagged" as being similar to the one used on the Brooklyn Cable R.R. I lost the note containing its length, but it was very long indeed.

) ;) ;) ;)

Thursday, Aug. 24.   This was Illinois Day and the attendance numbered 244,000. I saw the Midway Parade (Fig. 144), which was a very odd and noisy affair. Afterwards, I watched the Illinois State Military Parade (Fig. 145). A person near by said that there were eight thousand in line,

Fig. 144. Midway parade. Illinois Day.

Fig. 145. Illinois State Military parade. Joss House and tethered balloon exhibit on the right.

Fig. 146. Midway parade. Bicycle squad.

and I didn't doubt it; for I didn't see the
beginning of it, and I stood for a very long
time waiting for the end. It was composed of
Infantry, Cavalry, and Artillery. There were
some squads on bicycles (Fig. 146) also. Several
bands were in the line, but it was not a

Fig. 147. Esquimau villagers. Their village was a Labrador trading post and native exhibit.
Admission was 25¢.

Fig. 148. California Building. Old mission architecture, 435 feet long.

particularly fine looking line; for the day was very warm, and the line of march being very long didn't help the matter. I entered a few State Buildings this morning as I was up among them on my way to the Esquimau Village (Fig. 147). California (Fig. 148) had a fine lot of jars filled

Fig. 149. The life-sized Prune Horse from Santa Clara County, California, attracted wide general notice.

with her luscious fruit; even though she had a very large nice exhibit in the Horticultural Building. There was of course a nice display of oranges, and a horse

Fig. 150. The South Dakota Building, 70 x 126 feet, was covered in Yankton cement in imitation of stone work.

Fig. 151. The rotunda of the South Dakota Building with its exhibit of grains, petrified wood, and ores.

and rider made of prunes (Fig. 149) was an attractive monument in one part of the building. I have noted down in my book: "Large jars of little white onions." I think they must have looked very appetizing and nice at the time to have made me note them down.

South Dakota Building (Fig. 150) had some exhibits of furs and tin ores (Fig. 151).

Fig. 152. Nebraska Building, classical architecture of Corinthian order, 100 feet wide.

Nebraska had many cereal decorations in her home (Fig. 152).

The Kansas Building (Fig. 153) also had cereal decorations. A large case of cocoons and silk was an unexpected exhibit here. A small express train (Fig. 154) made frequent trips around the gallery of the rotunda. A particularly attractive feature was the forest

Fig. 153. Kansas Building, 135 x 138 feet in an irregular pattern.

Fig. 154. Rock Island model train exhibit in the rotunda of the Kansas Building.

Fig. 155. Animal panorama in the Kansas Building. By Professor Dyche, Kansas University.

scene (Fig. 155), which contained the wild
animals of Kansas and North America. I should

think that there were at least 100 mounted specimens. The space was fitted up as a section of forest, and the different animals were placed as they would be found in their native haunts. The principal animals were the moose (two bucks were fighting and had locked horns), deer, fox, rabbits, mountain goat, wolverine, wolf (several of these were mounted with their heads turned up and barking and were alive except for the bark), puma, buffalo, bear, elk, and a very finely mounted horse.

Texas had a very comfortable place for her visitors (Fig. 156). The picture of the

Fig. 156. The Texas Building was built with monies raised by the Women's World's Fair Exhibit Association when the state did not appropriate funds. A lone star and longhorn steer skull decorate the entrance.

Fig. 157. Portrait of Sam Houston on his horse was displayed in the Texas Building. The furnishings were created from the natural woods of Texas.

illustrious Sam Houston, of course, was found here (Fig. 157).

The Esquimau Village is worthy of a visit, but was not exceedingly interesting (Fig. 158). The men and women, the dogs, and an imitation of their half-spherical snow huts, I remember about. Three or four of the men Esquimaux were engaged in snapping coins (Fig. 159) from the earth with their long whips or walrus lariats with which they are very dexterous.

I thought I would meet Father in the center of the Manufactures Building at noon, but through a misunderstanding, I didn't meet him for he was in the center of the

Fig. 158. At this location, Esquimau Village huts were constructed of sheets of bark.

Fig. 159. Esquimau Village coin snappers.

Government Building instead. In the center of
the big Manufactures Building (Fig. 160) there
is a large tower (Fig. 161) under which is a monument (Fig. 162) covered with Columbian Souvenir
Half-dollars, and in the tower there are
chiming bells. These chimed "How Can I Leave

Fig. 160. The imposing southwest entrance to the Manufactures Building with its 80-foot archway. The ceilings of all four pavilion entrances to the building were ornamented with allegorical figures symbolic of arts and sciences.

Fig. 161. The Clock Tower, located in the center of the Manufactures Building, was 125 feet high and 40 feet square. A chime of bells surmounted the 7-foot-diameter clock, which was manufactured by the Self-winding Clock Company.

Fig. 162. An obelisk (left) covered with Columbian half-dollars was located in the center of the above Clock Tower. These silver half-dollars (inset) were the first commemorative coins minted by the U.S. Government. Actual size.

Thee" while I was around that afternoon, and it brought me back to the school days just past. Tiffany & Co. (Fig. 163), of course, had an elegant display; an ecclesiastical room (Fig. 164) was one of the features, but, someway, I didn't enjoy this display as much as lots of others.

Fig. 163. Tiffany & Company exhibit in Manufactures Building.

Fig. 164. Tiffany & Company's ecclesiastical room.

Fig. 165. Waterbury Watch Company exhibit. Manufactures Building.

A silver firm
showed the
different stages
in the manufac-
turing of spoons,
knives, and
forks, which
enlightened me
somewhat in that
business. A large
and very intri-
cate clock in the
Waterbury Watch
Co.'s booth
(Figs. 165 & 166),
showed marvelous

Fig. 166. Section of the Century Clock by Waterbury Watch Company with figurines of people working at various tasks.

genius in its make up. In the three or four stories of the piece, were figurines of people working at their different branches of trade: weaving, smithing, sewing, and other branches which I have forgotten.

In the Gallery the big publishing firms have their show. In general, they contain the principal publications of each exhibitor, and a large number of original manuscripts of noted contributors. Harpers' (Fig. 167) most notable exhibit was the original copy of "Ben Hur" by Lew Wallace. The Century Company showed how pictures are made (Fig. 168). Among a lot of original writings of noted men, was Lincoln's proclamation of 1861 for seventy-five thousand men, and several of Gen. U.S. Grant's letters. U.S. Card Co. had an exhibition too. Among the foreign educational exhibits, I found a

Fig. 167. Harpers Publishing Company exhibit in Manufactures Building Gallery.

Fig . 168. The Century Company's printing exhibit. Manufactures Building Gallery.

bookkeeping book in Japanese interesting.
Finding my way, at last, to my own State's
exhibit in that line, I found after much time
& looking the books containing the work of
the Olean Schools (Fig. 169). I felt as tho' I
had met an old school chum, and I spent quite

Fig. 169. New York Education exhibit. Included Olean. Manufactures, Liberal Arts, Gallery.

a time here especially in the age column of
the specimens. Rochester Business University
(Fig. 170) had a display of their school books
and pictures of their rooms among the other
business college exhibits.

Fig. 170. New York Education exhibit. Universities, including Rochester. Liberal Arts.

Fig. 171. Remington Pavilion
in Manufactures. The first
Columbian half-dollar is
encased and displayed on the
pole at the front of the exhibit
(arrow). Remington paid
$10,000 for the first coin
struck.

In the
Remington Type-
writers' booth
(Fig. 171), was
the $10,000
first Columbian
half-dollar
coined. This was
suspended in a
circular glass

disk enclosed by a brass border; this hinged on a similar cover (Fig. 172). A Columbian guard watches over this constantly (Fig. 173).

Fig. 172. The first Columbian half-dollar in its hinged brass holder. It was displayed in the Remington Pavilion and is now held by the Field Museum Library, Chicago.

Fig. 173. Columbian Guards assigned to the Manufactures Building. This elite corp numbered 2000 and was commanded by Col. Edmund Rice, U.S. Army. The uniform consisted of light-blue cloth ornamented with black braid and brass buttons.

The forty-inch Yerkes telescope (Fig. 174) on the main floor, which was dedicated the day before, showed the sort of instruments star gazers use. It is the largest instrument of its

Fig. 174. Charles T. Yerkes' 40-inch refracting telescope installed in the Manufactures Building. Today it is located at Lake Geneva, Wisconsin.

kind in the world. The Sapolio exhibit contained the famous boat "Sapolio," about fourteen feet long, in which Capt. Andrews sailed across the Atlantic in sixty days (Fig. 175). It was a heavily built boat, and was deep in proportion to its length. It looked as though all the room was made use of. A princely chamber suite was a beautiful exhibition in another place.

Fig. 175. Captain William A. Andrews on his dory, *Sapolio*, in Spain after sailing from Atlantic City, New Jersey, in 63 days to serve as a U.S. delegate to the Madrid Exposition of 1892. The next year at the World's Columbian Exposition, he and the boat were on exhibit at the north end of the Manufactures Building. Sapolio was the brand name of a soap.

<pre>
    ( ) ( ) ( ) ( ) ( ) ( )
)))))))))
))))))
        (((((
) ( )
</pre>

Friday, Aug. 25. Took the Ill. Central (Fig. 176) this morning to look over the town and secure advance tickets for the "America" (Fig. 177) at the Auditorium. Here, there was a long procession bent on the same errand, and one just plunks down what they ask and gets a

Fig. 176. The Illinois Central World's Fair trains at Van Buren in Chicago's business district.

Fig. 177. Program cover for Imre Kiralfy's "America" at the Auditorium on Michigan Avenue, Chicago.

ticket. The position which this commands in the house he is totally ignorant of; it may be way back a mile or so or up a couple of seats from the orchestra. Ours happened to be about midway, and were excellent. You also had to suit yourself to the dates upon which all the tickets were not sold. Father just happened to get a couple for Monday evening; later in the season, it was said that all these seats were sold a week or so in advance. After promenading about a bit, during which I, farmerlike, counted the stories of several skyscrapers, each numbering somewheres about ten, twelve, fifteen, and the 22-story one, her Highness the Masonic Temple, we came to the Board of Trade (Fig. 178). Going up in the public gallery, you look upon a large

Fig. 178. Chicago Board of Trade on Jackson.

floor, which was here and there dotted with a huddle of men shouting out unintelligible harangues, tho' I suppose that these same

seemingly unintelligible expressions trans-
ferred immense quantities of grain and hogs.
The uninitiated might at first sight imagine
that a big prize fight was about to take
place, and the sports had neglected to make
their bets until the last minute, and all
were now trying to make them—or you might
conceive a sheriff and posse causing a
similar scene at such a performance in tell-
ing what the Governor had said. After all,
there is a business air about it, and the
incessant ticking of innumerable telegraph
instruments together with the yellow message
fragments strewn about the floor, helped to
make civilization apparent.

The Masonic Temple (Fig. 179) was next
examined. Twenty-two rows of windows,
surrounded with brick and mortar, is what a
person counts from the pavement below. Just
inside the main entrance is the grand court,
or better the grand chute; for to a person
standing under it, it seems as though he were
looking up through an immense pipe or spout.
Elevators, a dozen or so, line one side of
it, and there is no waiting to get a lift;
the main difficulty being to decide which
will be the favored elevator. As you go up,
up, up, counting 12, 13, etc. numbers of the

different floors, you at last arrive at the twentieth where you pur- chase tickets for a quarter, and walk up to the observatory. Stability seemed to have impressed the architect very deeply in the construction of the huge building as shown by the iron stairways, marble walls and floors.

Fig. 179. The Masonic Temple at State and Randolph was 265 feet in height, one foot higher than the Ferris Wheel.

It was a beautiful August afternoon, as we stood gazing off on the immense city. Of course, we were above all, but some of the buildings close by met us quite a bit over halfway. The smoke of countless stacks spoiled the view in some directions, but there were acres of blocks of brick and mortar not out of sight. The Lake, dotted here and there by boats, lay with its beautiful blue waters off to the east. Two water works stations could be seen far out in the Lake. The broad boulevards lined with large trees outlined the way to the different parks of the city, which were square or rectangular patches of green in the distance. After our sightseeing here, and getting dinner, we hastened back and spent the afternoon on the Midway; about which I will tell later.

Fig. 180. The Woman's Building, 400 feet long, was located west of Wooded Island. Designed by Sophia Hayden in Italian renaissance style.

Saturday, Aug. 26. The Woman's Building (Fig. 180) was first visited by me this morning. Here in great display was fancy work, laces (Fig. 181), and dress goods. The useful patents by women (Fig. 182) were exhibited in one section. A very large book labeled the largest in the world attracted my attention. Several paintings (Fig. 183) showed what skill feminine hands had in that line. Taking all in all, I was not very much interested in this exhibition.

Fig. 181. Belgian lace exhibit in the Woman's Building.

Fig. 182. Patent Section for the inventions of women. Woman's Building.

Fig. 183. One of the art exhibits in the Woman's Building.

The Children's Building (Fig. 184) was very neat in its outside architecture; being in harmony with its occupants. Inside, the visitor

Fig. 184. The Children's Building was 150 feet long and three stories. The exterior was plain, as the only decoration was a blue painted frieze and eight medallions of children.

Fig. 185. The gymnasium in the Children's Building. This early form of daycare was considered one of the finer aspects of the Columbian Exposition.

could view through glass partitions children playing and under the care of nurses (Fig. 185).

Puck had a very neat little building of its own (Fig. 186). It principally showed the art of lithographing and does so by printing "Puck." Several presses are required in the operation; each in its turn adding an additional color print.

The Japanese buildings (Fig. 187) which are located on the north end of Wooded Island, are to be given to the City of Chicago after the Exposition by the Japanese Government. They were made after the manner of buildings in that country. Mattings covered the floors and the walls and ceilings were decorated in Japanese style (Fig. 188).

Fig. 186. The Puck Building, located between the Woman's and Horticultural buildings, was a parallelogram in form. From this building, the popular *Puck* magazine was printed in color during the Exposition.

Fig. 187. The Japan Building on Wooded Island was also called Ho-o-den or Phoenix Temple. It consisted of three connected buildings each in a different Japanese historical style. According to the Japanese method, the buildings were constructed of unpainted wood and the roofs were covered with sheet copper.

Fig. 188. One of the interior rooms of the Japan Building.

Walking quite a piece, I entered the Government Building (Fig. 189). A number of

Fig. 189. The Government Building faced the Lagoon and covered an area of 350 x 420 feet; the 120-foot in diameter central dome peaked at 150 feet.

ancient plows (Fig. 190) used in ancient countries were of great interest, there were of course many styles but none near so substantial or useful as a modern one; some being made entirely of wood. In the Patent Office Department one is lost in the innumerable

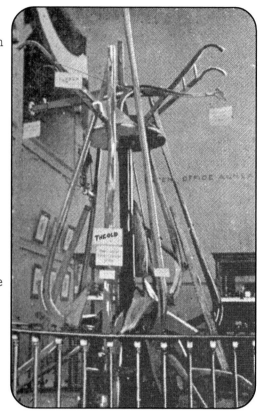

Fig. 190. Ancient plow exhibit in the Government Building. A small portion of the Patent Office exhibit is observable in the background.

models there exhibited. Hoe's presses were noticeable, and then there were a number of firearms. Steering equipments for steamers, thrashing machines, Deering self-binders, and many other noted inventions. In the fishing tackle display was a funny figure of a Negro. The model was entitled "Still Fishing," the Negro (Fig. 191) being asleep and a fish on his line. Under the large handsome dome of this building is a section of a California redwood

Fig. 191. "Still Fishing." Government Building exhibit.

Fig. 192. Redwood exhibit (below) in the rotunda of the Government Building. The rotunda paintings seen in the background are currently on display in the Columbian Theater, Wamego, Kansas.

about thirty feet high and twenty feet in diameter (Fig. 192). It was hollowed out and had been brought in small sections and afterwards placed in its natural position. Another tree was of much historical interest; it being known to be a seedling when Columbus first landed over here by actual count of rings. The War Department (Fig. 193) had a very complete display. A very interesting part of it was the manufacture of rifles and cartridges. A machine bored the barrels and over in another place the stocks were going through a shaping machine. About a dozen different machines were used in the manufacture of a loaded shell. The first one merely punched circular pieces about the size

Fig. 193. War Department Exhibit. Torpedo in center foreground. Government Building.

of a nickel out of a sheet of brass. The next shapes it; the next draws it out in length and so on—the bullets being made in one—the cartridges in another, and finally all put together. Several cannons were exhibited, both modern and some that did notable service in the late war. A section of a tree shot into (Fig. 194), and one that had been shot off were also historic relics of that war. A torpedo boat was of interest; every little while its screw would revolve rapidly showing that it could command great

Fig. 194. Chickamauga Bullet Tree from the U.S. Civil War. Gnarls from growth over embedded bullets on all sides are shown in this mirror reflection. Government Building.

speed. Figures dressed in military uniform (Fig. 195) illustrating the different ranks were very lifelike, indeed so much so that I imagine more than one addressed them in good faith.

Fig. 195. Lifelike figures of General Schofield and staff in uniform. Government Building.

The Smithsonian Institution (Fig. 196) had
a very large exhibit in the Government Building.
A large number of mounted birds and animals
were interesting and instructive; and then
there was a great lot of pretty butterflies.

Fig. 196. The Smithsonian exhibit. Government Building.

Fig. 197.   Coast Guard exhibit. Government Building.

A number of dried tobacco leaves showed what the original form of the cigars were. Hemp and flax were exhibited in their different stages of manufacture into ropes and cords of which there were a number of samples. A quarter of beef and a side of hog made of wax were very clever in their close resemblance to the real articles. Insects and small animals made in artificial form of large size were of interest to the student. The Coast Defense (Fig. 197) part contained several lamps for lighthouses; some of which were immense in size. The Mint exhibit (Fig. 198) near by was of course of great interest. There, a regular minting machine could be seen in operation turning out souvenir coins

Fig. 198. United States Mint exhibit. Government Building. In the background the large "Coast Defense" lighthouse lenses in the nearby Coast Guard exhibit are seen.

Fig. 199. Brass Columbian Exposition Treasury Department medal. Reverse and Obverse. Stamped in the Government Building.

of the Building (Fig. 199), which were about the size of a dollar. The exhibit contained some bills of rather high denomination. A couple of fives and a ten thousand dollar bank note looked exceedingly inviting. An extensive display of

old coins was also here; one being the oldest
known coin.

The Post Office Department had a complete
display, showing the advance made from the old
mail coach to the modern mail car palace (Fig.
200). An appliance was attached to a car which
took mail sacks along the road while the train
is in motion. A complete set of Columbian
stamps, a post office (Fig. 201) in full operation,

Fig. 200. The "Benjamin Harrison" Railway Mail Car exhibit, a 70-foot-long car, was fully
manned by railway mail clerks demonstrating how mail was sorted at 60 miles per hour.

Fig. 201. Official World's Fair Post Office. Specially canceled mail delivered from this office,
a branch of the Chicago Post Office, is highly prized today. The "Dead Letter Office" was one
of the many displays. Government Building.

having the business of the grounds, and some
samples of the articles that find their way
to the Dead Letter Office were of interest. Of
these dead letter curios I note a few: birds'
eggs, bootblack box, baseball, stuffed elephant,
coconut, perfume, Chinese writings, raisins,
an accordion, fruitcake or plum pudding, lamp,
seed corn, cups, shoes, stirrups, shells, combs,
telegraph instruments, tea pot, old coins,
butter ladle, roller skates, chisels, horseshoes,
halter, snakes in bottle, brick, whip, alligator, stuffed birds, revolver, ax, umbrella,
saw, lamp chimney, etc., etc., etc., etc.

Benjamin Franklin's ledger was connected
with the P.O. Dep't, I guess. It looked very
neat, and dated back in the 1770s.

Sunday, Aug. 27.

We didn't get around in very good season
this morning for it was Sunday, but after
breakfast we decided to take a walk up in
Washington Park (Fig. 202). The weather was quite
warm and we found it very agreeable walking
under the shade of the trees as we went from
the lower to the upper end of the park where
the large beautiful flower beds are. There is
quite a large lake down in the lower part of
the grounds and some flowers, but the northern
part is where the fine flowers are. The park

Fig. 202. Lovers' Lake in Washington Park just west of the Midway.

is traversed by wide paved drives. On our way
we found no signs "Keep off the Grass," but
instead, people lying in the shade of trees,
reading, sleeping, and some from the near by
houses had brought hammocks and were taking
considerable comfort. Tennis courts by the
dozen were laid out in one quarter. The flower
beds lay on top and at the sides of a large
mound about six feet high with a gentle slope.
Around the foot were geranium beds all red with
blossoms, tuber roses, roses, canna, and a
deep purple flower, which was very pretty.
Around on the sides of the mound were beds laid
out particularly in regard to shape. Different
colored foliaged plants formed a horseshoe,

with a four leafed clover in the center, an
anchor, cross, the treble staff was outlined
and contained half a dozen notes; above this
was written "Hail Columbia." Rolls of carpet
with a yard or two unrolled were outlined in
the same manner. All this work looked very
beautiful; for it was done in a very artistic
manner, and it was trimmed so that neatness
and uniformity prevailed. Several urns, or you
might call them huge vases, showed remarkable
pains in this line. These, as well as some of
the others I mention, were covered with a spe-
cies of cactus, a plant very flat and about three
inches in diameter. It had a light slaty color.
Wide steps with a matting pictured in the center, led up to a large gateway (Fig. 203), which

Fig. 203. Cactus Garden steps and gate. Washington Park.

Fig. 204. "Sol's Clock," a sundial in Washington Park. Plant urns in the background.

was made with the aid of the plants I have just tried to describe. Old Sol's clock was a striking piece of landscape gardening (Fig. 204). The hand consisted of an immense cactus, about eight feet long, a foot in diameter, slanting towards the North, I think. The numbers from one to twelve were about it in a semicircle. We were looking at it ten minutes before twelve and the shadow of the hand lay slightly at the left of the twelve. A large sphere had the continents outlined upon it (Fig. 205). Pretty ornamental borders intertwined among the different beds. On the farther side is the greenhouse and a pond for water plants. Many pond lilies were in bloom in the latter place, and many torrid plants grew there. The oddest variety was the Victoria Regia, a plant with a large leaf like a water lily, only the edge was turned up perpendicularly

Fig. 205. The living globe in the Washington Park Cactus Garden.

Fig. 206. Victoria Regia plants in the Washington Park lily pond.

to the surface (Fig. 206). It is said that in their most luxuriant state they can hold a child, but I should hate to risk many pair of any other than old shoes on these. An Egyptian lotus was beautifully in bloom. The greenhouse contained many interesting plants including a banana tree with a ripe bunch, date palms, palms, tree ferns, orchids, large vines, cactus, and other things so that it looked as though the park people had borrowed a few of the shipments to the Horticultural Building down on the Fair Grounds.

Buffalo Bill's Wild West Show (Fig. 207) is a great show for a paleface. It is held in a large arena with the seats under cover at the three sides; the remaining side being the entrance and occupied by a large curtain typical

Fig. 207. Buffalo Bill's Wild West Show cast of characters, Chicago, 1893. Buffalo Bill, wearing a white hat, is standing before the tent; Annie Oakley is in front of him.

Fig. 208. Buffalo Bill's "Rough Riders." The Show was located just outside the fairgrounds between 62nd and 63rd Streets and Grace and Hope Avenues.

of the performance. The show is advertised to take place twice daily, rain or shine. The

Fig. 209. Annie Oakley, sharp-shooter. By J.J. Gibson, World's Fair Official Photographer.

soft black dirt of the arena is raked smooth before the performance. Bands of men mounted on horses represented the military of the different nations of the world. Reckless riding, riding bucking broncos (Fig. 208), an old-time stagecoach robbery, crack shooting (Fig. 209), great feats of juggling, races, tricks on horseback, and many other incidents kept one's mind from wandering very far off. A curious thing was an Arabian, who kept turning around, by holding one foot still and walking the body around with the other. This he kept up for it must have been ten minutes. The terrible slaughter of Gen. Custer at the Battle Of Little Big Horn was the closing panorama. It was pictured out in all its minutest details; the horses playing dead in a very natural manner.

Monday, Aug. 28. I went to the Fine Arts Building (Fig. 210) to finish it, and it was noon before I could leave it. I went through all, but that is about all I can say of it; for in looking at so many and doing it so quickly,

Fig. 210. Fine Arts Building, south entrance facing North Pond.

one can but have a confused memory of the pictures he has seen. There were so many of them,
room after room lined with them, and those who
could take different visits to it were the
fortunate ones. The pictures I particularly
noticed and remembered on this trip are in the
list with those of the first trip.

Fig. 211. The Roof Walkway was well over one-half mile around and 240 feet above grade.
There were 30 staircases to the main floor, each 12 feet wide. A small portion of 11 acres of
glass skylights are seen on the left. Manufactures Building.

After lunch at Wellington's in the
Manufactures Building, I took a walk around
the roof of this building (Fig. 211). Here, as
on the Masonic Temple or Ferris Wheel, you
are way up. This walk will stay in memory for
many years to come for everything below looked
very beautiful this pleasant sunny afternoon.

The blue waters of Lake Michigan on one side, Wooded Island, the state buildings and the Midway in the distance with the Ferris Wheel (Fig. 212) as a distinguishing feature, all made grand scenes long to be remembered. A visitor can only reach the roof by elevator (Fig. 213)

Fig. 212. Ferris Wheel. The Fair's most recognizable icon, located in the middle of the Midway Plaisance, was the creation of bridge engineer George W. G. Ferris.

and after going around descends to the gallery by flights of stairs which run down each corner of the building. On largely attended days, guards see that you keep moving. This precaution is to keep the roof from being overcrowded, and is very necessary in case the roof needs to be cleared quickly on account of some accident, four elevators being insufficient for doing this. Fire protection in the way of water attachments with short pieces of

Fig. 213. Hale Elevator Company's four cars to the roof of Manufactures Building carried occupants 220 feet up for 50¢.

hose and pails of water was abundant around the top. On each corner there is an immense search light (Fig. 214). From the ground they look like the headlights of an ordinary locomotive, but close to them, they tower above one's head. The glass in one of them I think was said to be five feet in diameter, and was in narrow parallel parts. The carbons were I judge three times the size of the ordinary arc ones. The "Scientific American" in describing the largest one says that it can be seen in Milwaukee, eighty miles distant, on a

Fig. 214. A giant searchlight on the Roof Walkway of Manufactures Building.

Fig. 215. The electric arc searchlight on the deck of the battleship *Illinois* exhibit. The Illinois Building is seen in the background.

Fig. 216. The gilt "Statue of the Republic,"
designed by Daniel Chester French, stood 100 feet
above the water of the Grand Basin. French is best
known for his Lincoln in the Lincoln Memorial.

favorable night, and further says that a man can read a newspaper eight miles away by its aid. These together with some on the neighboring buildings and the two on the "Illinois" battleship (Fig. 215) play about the grounds during the evening, shining now and then on the lofty figures of the buildings and making them look of glistening whiteness. The golden statue of the Republic (Fig. 216) also receives attention, as does the Ferris Wheel down the Midway. As they make a light streak for some distance, they sometimes cross each other and outline a cross or square in the darkness. Descending this lofty perch which I well remembered as being very windy for a good stiff breeze was

Fig. 217. The whaleback *Christopher Columbus* transported World's Fair visitors between Long Pier at the Exposition and a pier near the Chicago business district. It was operated by the World's Fair Steamship Company, and a round-trip ticket cost 25¢.

blowing in from the Lake, I hastened to meet Father on the pier to take the whaleback "Christopher Columbus," (Fig. 217) to the city to attend "America." Father, in the meantime, had looked up Jack Decker and the two were walking as I came up. The water looked pretty rough to them to take the trip, and it looked choppy as an old sailor would say. After Father had made an engagement with Jack to meet us at the Casino (Fig. 218) for dinner the following day, we started for the city by rail and found the whaleback moored up there, not making any trips on account of the stormy waters. We again took a good look at the business part of town which seemed very dirty as frequent gusts of wind would blow the dust

Fig. 218. The Casino, 140 x 260 feet and located at the south end of the Peristyle, was operated by the Bureau of Public Comfort and became a favorite resort for visitors.

Fig. 219. Erie Lines advertisement with route map from Chicago to Buffalo and on to New York City. The left-side illustration is of "I Will," which remains a Chicago trademark.

about. Father purchased return tickets at the Erie's (Fig. 219) uptown ticket office and I had sent from a bookstore a book about the

Exposition to Aunt Allie. The restaurant we took supper in was lined on the sides and ceiling with plate mirrors, so that it looked acres in extent as we entered. However we ate just as much and it set just as well, if there were illusions all about us. Before going to the theater, we stepped into the Auditorium Hotel and found it very beautiful (Fig. 220). The Opera House is a magnificent affair (Fig. 221). The upholstered seats and pure ventilation made it comfortable sitting. Two rows of boxes were on each side, about thirty or forty in all. It was lit by electricity, and this was

Fig. 220. The Auditorium is still located on the corner of Michigan Avenue and Congress Street. In 1893 it was America's "most famous building" with its grand opera house, hotel, and business offices. There are ten floors in the main building.

Fig. 221. The Auditorium stage. The auditorium was on the first floor and had a permanent seating capacity of 4000; for conventions it could hold 8000.

regulated so that it could be turned up or down. Now for the show: It is what I think is called a spectacular production. A large number take part in it (Fig. 222); all of which are dressed in brilliant costumes decorated with many yards of gold braid and silver

Fig. 222. Production number from act three of "America" at the Auditorium Opera House.

buttons (Fig. 223).
Tableaus and
scenes represent-
ing Columbus at
different inter-
vals on his
voyage were nice
productions.
Horses as well as
men took part.
The Mutiny on
Board was
represented by a
large boat made
up in the old

Fig. 223. "America": Progress, Bigotry, and Liberty.

style which rocked up and down very naturally,
and the occupants played mutiny. There was a
great deal of dancing intermingled all through
it, making it resemble a kirmess. Some great
things in the slight-of-hand line were
introduced as specialties and were pleasing
variations. Here are a few examples: keep
three very unequal articles in the air by
tossing and catching, take two things in one
hand in the same way and wave a silk hat
between them, balance a common breakfast
plate on a horse whip, and this on a lighted
cigar, keep a heavy wagon wheel revolving on
the end of a small pole, set a glass of water

in a hoop and swing it around the head, various feats with eggs, and many difficult things in tumbling. The principal man in the latter held up seven or eight of the others. The exits of the house were many and very convenient.

- : : : : : : : : : : -

Fig. 224. Lake Michigan Beach looking north. Manufactures Building on the left.

Tuesday, Aug. 29. I spoke of the waters being so rough that the whaleback did not make her usual trips yesterday afternoon. This morning, when we went out on the lake-front by the Manufactures Building, we found that the water had been stormy during the night and was quite angry yet. There was much evidence of this by the wreckage along shore; most of which was the fireworks pier. It seemed quite the thing this morning to go down on the beach (Fig. 224) and poke in the sand for pretty pebbles, so we went with the rest and filled a pocket with this kind of souvenir. We took another trip in the big building and were interested in looking at a great wealth of

Fig. 225. Elaborate American cut-glass display. Manufactures Building.

fine glassware (Fig. 225). We found the beautiful little statue in the Italian Section (Fig. 226) which Mr. Rogers purchased. It was the figure of a little girl sewing. To Mr. Rogers' card

Fig. 226. Entrance to the Italian Section. Manufactures Building.

Fig. 227. Interior of the Casino. The popular Casino Restaurant was on the second floor.

Fig. 228. The Mammoth Exhibit, provided by Ward's Natural Science Establishment, Rochester, New York, occupied the entire south gallery of the Anthropological Building.

were the cards of twenty or more other pur-
chasers. At noon, we took dinner at the Casino
(Fig. 227) with Jack, and afterwards I went down
to the southern part of the grounds, mainly to
visit the gallery of the Anthropological Building, which was interesting with its stuffed
animals, coins, and birds' eggs, the largest
and smallest of which lay side by side. A huge
mammoth was made up in its natural form (Fig.
228). The rest of the p.m. was spent in taking
farewell glimpses about the grounds; we stayed
quite late this evening.

Wednesday, Aug. 30. We hustled our
baggage, and souvenirs together this morning

and about one p.m. started via the Erie
homeward bound. For some time we could catch
glimpses of the vanishing White City. Our car
was the "Thackeray" and we had a pleasant
trip in it home with little incident.

-)))))(((((-

THE MIDWAY -:- THE MIDWAY -:- THE MIDWAY

This side show of the Great Fair has
spread its fame far over the land. The several
nationalities are planted side by side in this
one street; a shop of some country; a theater
of another; a castle of another and so on,
until nearly all the great countries of the
world have a spot ornamented with some building typical of its native land. A number of
people of the different countries were here to
see after their several interests and made the
place the more strange. Some well call it a
wild scene as they walk down it at night. The
people in their native costumes bustling to
and fro; shop venders and coachers to the many
theaters and side attractions fill the air
with their yells. And, of course, one hears a
different language at every step. Music is an
essential part to nearly every establishment
and varies from a well-trained German Band

Fig. 229. The Imperial German Infantry Band. The Royal Director was E. Ruschewcyh, standing center behind front row. German Village, Midway Plaisance.

Fig. 230. A Turkish Theater drummer. Midway Plaisance.

(Fig. 229) to the rat-a-tat-tat of the Turks (Fig. 230). All this bedlam is going on under the bright glare of electric lights and a jolly crowd of visitors passing up and down. It

Fig. 231. The Electric Scenic Theater where colored light bulbs were used to produce scenic effects for "A Day in the Alps." Admission was 25¢.

mattered little what might be the attractions elsewhere, the Midway would always be thronged; its busy time, however, being during the p.m. on 'til midnight. Necessarily walking down the street a ways to the hotel, we would take a tramp down the whole length nearly every night, stopping at a new place of attraction or so each trip. Our first place was a disappointment for a beginning. It was styled the Electric Scenic Theater (Fig. 231). After gazing for a short time at a small view of the Alps to the accompaniment of a piano, doors were opened at the sides and "exit" yelled so that the place might be cleared for duping more people. Blarney Castle (Fig. 232) and a collection of Irish

Fig. 232. The Blarney Castle exhibit reproduced the 15th Century original. Ascending the winding staircase a visitor could creep to the battlements and kiss the magic stone.

Fig. 233. Irish Village Industries. Fee 25¢. Blarney Castle was located on these grounds too.

Fig. 234. The Libbey Glass Company exhibit entrance on the Midway. Admission was 10¢.

Industries (Fig. 233) afforded little interest to me. The castle I judge might be a good

reproduction but after going up countless flights of stairs you reach the top of the structure only to look at merely a Chicago paving brick which was styled, however, the Blarney Stone. A fee is charged for kissing it. The Libbey Glass Company (Fig. 234)

Fig. 235. Eulalia's glass dress woven by Libbey Glass.

Fig. 236. Glass
weaving looms at the
Libbey Glass exhibit.
(Left)

Fig. 237. Libbey's
glass-melting furnace
and base of its
tapering stack, which
rose through the
center of the building
to a height of 100 feet.
(Below)

made a very large
display in glassware.
One department was
devoted to cut glass,
another to articles
woven of glass, neck-
ties, mats, and the
dress made for the
Princess Eulalia,
were exhibited (Fig.
235). Several girls
in another section
were spinning the
glass, and weaving
it (Fig. 236). A very
large chimney (Fig.
237) for making the

glass occupied the center of the building, and blowers were blowing glass pears for souvenirs. They made many other things for sale, such as paper weights with the pictures of the different fair buildings on the back (Fig. 238).

Fig. 238. Libbey Glass paperweight depicting the Illinois State Building. Their distinctive black and white designs were all printed with "Made at World's Fair by Libbey Glass Co. Patented." The bottoms are sealed with low-temperature milk glass.

The Javanese Village (Fig. 239) is a collection of native huts from that far off Eastern Island. They are made of bamboo and cane (Fig. 240). The dark-skinned natives were interesting, especially a very small youngster (Fig. 241). An orang-outang occupied a cage near the entrance.

Fig. 239. Inside the Java Village. The village contained the streets and houses of 125 natives from the Dutch East Indies. Admission was 10¢ to the village and 25¢ to their theater.

Fig. 240. Javanese hut and family in the Java Village, Midway Plaisance.

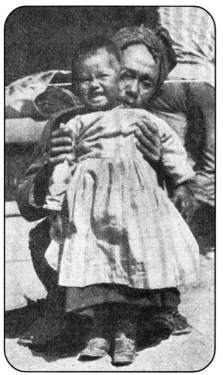

Fig. 241. The popular Javanese baby.

The South Sea Islanders (Fig. 242) gave their characteristic dances in a theater (Fig. 243) across the way, and great shakedowns they were. The men were finely physically developed, their chests, arms, and legs being bare (Fig. 244), you could see the perspiration stand out on their giant forms.

Fig. 242. South Sea Islanders. The village consisted of four native houses and 25 villagers. Admission 25¢.

Fig. 243. South Sea Island Theater. The islanders performed as often as every hour daily the songs and dances of Samoa, Fiji, Romutah, and Wallis Islands.

Fig. 244. Three Samoans from the Theater. This photo illustrates their fine physical condition. Two would go out on the Midway and advertise an upcoming performance. The Islanders all gathered together and sang "America" in their native tongue at the end of each performance.

Filippo, Samoan Giant Chief (inset) by J.J. Gibson, Official Photographer.

Fig. 245. Switzerland's Panorama of the Bernese Alps. The viewpoint was from the Maennlichen's 7700-foot elevation. Admission 50¢.

-###########-

The Panorama of the Bernese Alps was a good production (Fig. 245). As you stood on a high platform in the center of the round build-ing looking at the canvas around the outside, it seemed incredible that the canvas was only a few feet away in reality, instead of being several rods. It was also difficult to believe that it hung vertically. The mountains and the sheep on the mountains, the brook in the valley looked to be way, way down below us, and the cottage of some mountaineer stood out very naturally.

The German Village. I don't remember much about this place. I think there was a representation of an old castle with moat and draw bridge about it (Fig. 246). Cairo Street a little farther up, we entered one evening (Fig. 247). The street is lined on both sides with all kinds of shops where trinkets were for sale. This together with the Turkish Village (Fig. 248) and the Algerian settlement (Fig. 249) had mostly the same lot of trinkets. These consisted of many sandalwood articles, embroidered mats,

Fig. 246. German Village Castle surrounded by a 50-foot-wide water-filled moat. Admission to the Village was free, the museum inside was 25¢, and the concert garden was 25¢.

Fig. 247. Street in Cairo (above) was lined with 62 shops. Admission was 15¢ and two street processions were held each day. Cafes at the two ends of the street supplied light lunches served by native attendants. The "Danse du Ventre" (belly dance) was held in the theater, admission 25¢. There were many other charges, including 25¢ for a camel ride.

Fig. 248. Turkish Village admission was 25¢, admission to the mosque, a reproduction of the mosque built by Sultan Selim, was free.

Fig. 249. The Algerian and Tunisian Village consisted of several exhibits. The Algerian Theater, shown here, had an admission fee of 25¢. Their 50-booth bazaar was free.

Fig. 250. The grand Turkish Bazaar had 40 booths where goods peculiar to the country were sold. Admission was free.

Fig. 251. Camel rides were available at Street in Cairo and Turkish Village. Midway Plaisance.

all sorts of spoons, beads, foreign coins, candy and other things too numerous to mention (Fig. 250). The camel riding is indulged in by a number of visitors, but we just looked on and enjoyed the sport (Fig. 251). The theater

Fig. 252. Algerian Theater dancer. Algerian and Tunisian Village. Midway Plaisance.

performance in this place goes a good ways. A female goes through all sorts of movements to the rub-dub-dub on a queer-shaped drum played by a native (Fig. 252). We are now about to the Ferris Wheel, whose inventor became famous on account of the successful mounting, and the ability of this monster wheel to revolve (Fig. 253). The diameter is 250 feet and between its two outer rims are suspended thirty-six coaches (Fig. 254) capable of holding about two thousand people. In the evening, the wheel and its supporting towers are lit up and outlined by long rows of incandescent lights, so that it can

Fig. 253. View of the fairgrounds from the Ferris Wheel. Total height was 264 feet. A steam-driven metal link belt engaged cogs on the rim of the wheel. The center axle, made by Bethlehem Iron Co. and seen in this view, was the largest forged ironwork to that time.

be seen a long ways through the darkness. But our trip around it was taken one delightful afternoon. A better idea of its loftiness is given, and you also get a good view of things far and near. The Wheel is the most

Fig. 254. A single Ferris Wheel car was the size of a Pullman Palace car and upholstered just as luxuriously, each coach seating 40 persons plus a polite attendant. The drive cogs on the rim of the wheel are clearly seen in this view.

satisfactory thing on the Midway. The price of a ride was fifty cents for twice around (Fig. 255).

Fig. 255. Fifty-cent Ferris Wheel ticket.

The Moorish Palace (Fig. 256) was a very satisfactory visiting place on the Street. One part was devoted to illusions and a person had to keep his wits about him or he would go smack up against the cause of his discomfiture, the large mirrors which lined the place. A bottomless well constructed by the same aid was indeed bottomless, as far as

Fig. 256. Moorish Palace. Considered one of the better attractions on the Midway. Admission was 25¢ and included the Optical Illusion Theater.

I could see; for you could look what seemed to be way, way down out o' sight. Apart from this, for a nickel, you could see the place above or the opposite pictured out. A very interesting illusion was produced by lining the sides and ceiling of a three cornered room with mirrors. Although perhaps you were the sole occupant of the room there seemed to be hundreds about you, and, if you waved your hat, all of these illusive people did likewise, thus

Fig. 257. Many scenes with lifelike wax figurines were on display on the second floor of the Moorish Palace. Here, "Marie Antoinette" is being led to the guillotine that was used in her actual execution. A Columbian Guard stands to the right in this photograph.

producing an enormous cheer. Upstairs there are some excellent wax figures (Fig. 257), some of them were soldiers, but not all of them. Here were also some convex and concave mirrors about as tall as a person which distorted one looking into one of them. A beer garden in connection had ballet dancers and variety acting.

An ice railway (Fig. 258) put up by some ice machine concern afforded coasting in midsummer for those who cared for that pastime (Fig. 259).

Fig. 258. The Ice Railway Company track with powerhouse within its loop. Admission was 10¢ for two trips around the 875-foot track. De La Bergne refrigerating machinery made the ice and snow. Located near the Ferris Wheel and Moorish Palace. Midway Plaisance.

Fig. 259. View when sledding on the Ice Railway track. Each sled held 16 people. The ammonia refrigeration pipes were underneath the track.

Fig. 260. Austrian Village and Old Vienna. Old Vienna was an exact reproduction of that Vienna section called the "Graben" as it appeared 200 years prior to the Exposition. There were 70 shops, a bandstand, and the large and popular Vienna restaurant. Admission was 25¢.

Fig. 261. Professor C.M. Ziehrer (arrow) and his Royal Austrian Band played at Old Vienna, Midway Plaisance, every evening from five to ten, including Sunday, during the entire Fair.

Old Vienna (Fig. 260) was a delightful place and Father and I spent nearly an entire evening in it listening to the fine music of the large band (Fig. 261) and in looking over the different shops (Figs. 262 & 263). It was a beautiful evening, and seemed to me very

Fig. 262. Bohemian Glass Shop. One of the many shops in Old Vienna. Midway Plaisance.

Fig. 263. Bohemian Jewelry Shop specializing in garnet and gold. Old Vienna. Midway Plaisance.

romantic amid such surroundings (Fig. 264). The band played "Trovatore" and some beautiful waltzes while we were there.

- §§§§§§$$$$$ -

Fig. 264. An evening in Old Vienna on the Midway Plaisance included a delectable dinner, the enchanting music of Ziehrer's Austrian Band, and entertainment by the Night Watch (Valentine Peters) in period costume—all under the stars and the revolving illumination of the imposing Ferris Wheel. J.J. Gibson's official photograph of Peters is the inset.

"It was a beautiful evening, and seemed to me very romantic amid such surroundings."

Friend Pitts Williams
Age 18, August 1893

ACKNOWLEDGMENTS

Alan Aimone, Senior Librarian, U.S. Military Academy, West Point, New York

Marilyn LeGrys Decker, Troy, New York

Christopher Densmore, Librarian, Friends Library, Swarthmore College,
        Swarthmore, Pennsylvania

Tom Donahue, Olean Times Herald, Olean, New York

Betty Eaton, Olean Historical Society, Olean, New York

Adam Gorelick, Sandia Computers, Albuquerque, New Mexico

Richard Gould, Archivist, Houghton Academy, Houghton, New York

Leo John and Moira F. Harris, Pogo Press, St. Paul, Minnesota

Irene Williams Hartwig, Clarence Center, New York

Linda Kennedy, Buffalo and Erie County Historical Society, Buffalo, New York

Susan Kulp, Orchard Park Historical Society, Orchard Park, New York

Kenneth LeGrys, Cambridge, New York

Warren LeGrys, Mesa, Arizona

Barbara Lias, Principal, Olean High School, Olean, New York

Lesley Martin, Chicago Historical Society, Chicago, Illinois

Chuck Massaro, Olean Times Herald, Olean, New York

Ronald W. Nelson, Albuquerque, New Mexico

Charlotte Norwood, Manuscript Editor, Albuquerque, New Mexico

Susan S. Palmer, Archives Reference Librarian, Cornell University, Ithaca, New York

Cordell Puckett, Albuquerque, New Mexico

Katie Quinn, Reference Librarian, Albany Public Library, Albany, New York

Linda Rinella, Orchard Park Central School, Orchard Park, New York

Kathy Sheehan, Registrar, Rensselaer County Historical Society, Troy, New York

Kathy Sherburne, Olean Historical Society, Olean, New York

Brad Spink, President of Mount View Cemetery Association, Olean, New York

Kenneth B. Srail, Collector, North Olmstead, Ohio

Julie Stavish, Records Clerk, Olean High School, Olean, New York

Phillip Stockin, Headmaster, Houghton Academy, Houghton, New York

Ruth E. Sweet, Reference Librarian, Troy Public Library, Troy, New York

Lorraine Walsh, Reference Librarian, St. Bonaventure University, Allegany, New York

Numbers in parentheses are bibliographic citation numbers from *Annotated Bibliography : World's Columbian Exposition, Chicago 1893* by Dybwad and Bliss, 1992. Citations with decimal extenders are from our *Supplement*, 1999.

ILLUSTRATION SOURCES BY FIGURE NUMBER

4- Lake Shore RR timetable (907.2)
5- Klein p.409 (902)
8- *Pictorial Album* (1651)
9- WCE Columbus entrance ticket
10- Kilburn Stereocard #8201
11- *World's Fair Album* (1723)
12- *Halligan's Pictorial* (1623)
13- *Graphic.* 9.13: 249 (1449)
14- Johnson, v.3, p.329 (895)
15- Klein p.256 (902)
16- Klein p.254 (902)
17- Bancroft p.584 (733)
18- Klein p.309 (902)
19- *World's Fair Album* (1723)
20- Ropp. *W.F. Souvenir* (1662)
21- *Beautiful Scenes* (1575)
22- *Columbian Gallery* (1599)
23- Johnson, v.1, p.430 (895)
24- Johnson, v.1, p.483 (895)
25- Kilburn Stereocard #8720
26- Johnson, v.2, p.1 (895)
27- Ellis p.59 (836)
28- Ellis p.130 (836)
29- Ellis p.152 (836)
30- Bancroft p.403 (733)
31- Ellis p.160 (836)
32- Bancroft p.412 (733)
33- Ellis p.157 (836)
34- Ellis p.158 (836)
35- *World's Fair Album* (1723)
36- Bancroft p.427 (733)
37- *Columbian Gallery* (1599)
38- Bancroft p.435 (733)
39- Bancroft p.437 (733)
40- Campbell 3.12: 339 (1462)
41- *Reminiscences* (1660)
42- *World's Fair Album* (1723)
43- Ropp. *W.F. Souvenir* (1662)
44- Jenks p.219 (20)
45- Johnson, v.3, p.241 (895)
46- Bancroft p.588 (733)
47- Bancroft p.589 (733)
48- Bancroft p.600 (733)
49- Campbell 3.2: 60 (1462)
50- Naphtha Launch ad (850.4)
51- *World's Fair Album* (1723)
52- Bancroft p.530 (733)

53- Bancroft p.524 (733)
54- Bancroft p.523 (733)
55- Bancroft p.536 (733)
56- Ropp. *W.F. Souvenir* (1662)
57- *Reminiscences* (1660)
58- *World's Fair Album* (1723)
59- Shepp p.397 (1667)
60- *World's Fair Album* (1723)
61- Johnson v.2, p.486 (895)
62- Ropp. *W.F. Souvenir* (1662)
63- *Gems of the WF* (1616)
64- *Halligan's Pictorial* (1623)
65- Kurtz p.224 (907)
66- *Gems of the WF* (1616)
67- Kurtz p.237 (907)
68- Kurtz p.234 (907)
69- *Art and Artists* p.24 (1569)
70- *Art and Artists* p.197 (1569)
71- *World's Fair Album* (1723)
72- Johnson v.3, p.183 (895)
73- Johnson v.3, p.168 (895)
74- Shepp p.483 (1667)
75- Shepp p.449 (1667)
76- Ropp. *W.F. Souvenir* (1662)
77- *Columbian Gallery* (1559)
78- Johnson v.2, p.448 (895)
79- Bancroft p.803 (733)
80- Shepp p.369 (1667)
81- Bancroft p.798 (733)
82- *World's Fair Album* (1723)
83- Johnson v.3, p.481 (895)
84- *World's Fair Album* (1723)
85- *Columbian Gallery* (1559)
86- *Graphic.* 9.20:403 (1449)
87- New York State. plate at p.108 (1991)
88- Bancroft p.769 (733)
89- *World's Fair Album* (1723)
90- *Report of the Mass. Bd.* p.14 (1921)
91- *Columbian Gallery* (1559)
92- *Columbian Gallery* (1559)
93- Ropp. *W.F. Souvenir* (1662)
94- Klein p.298 (902)
95- *World's Fair Album* (1723)
96- Klein p.248 (902)
97- *Graphic* 9.13:247 (1449)
98- *Graphic* 9.13:286 (1449)
99- Bancroft p.907 (733)

100- Bancroft p.551 (733)
101- Bancroft p.553 (733)
102- Bancroft p.549 (733)
103- *Halligan's Pictorial* (1623)
104- Bancroft p.562 (733)
105- Bancroft p.579 (733)
106- Bancroft p.537 (733)
107- Shepp p.325 (1667)
108- Klein p.159 (902)
109- Shepp p.323 (1667)
110- *Columbian Gallery* (1599)
111- Bancroft p.489 (733)
112- Kilburn Stereocard #8594
113- *Reminiscences* (1660)
114- Bancroft p.474 (733)
115- *Columbian Gallery* (1599)
116- Ropp. *W.F. Souvenir* (1662)
117- *Halligan's Pictorial* (1623)
118- Johnson v.3, p.28 (895)
119- Bancroft p.347 (733)
120- Bancroft p.363 (733)
121- Bancroft p.364 (733)
122- Bancroft p.389 (733)
122 Inset-Authors' collection
123- Bancroft p. 603 (733)
124- Johnson, v.3, p.190 (895)
125- Bancroft p.646 (733)
126- Rose, plate facing p.44 (1662.1)
127- *Columbian Gallery* (1599)
128- *Reminiscences* (1660)
129- *World's Fair Album* (723)
130- *Beautiful Scenes* (1575)
131- Bancroft p.453 (733)
132- Bancroft p.460 (733)
133- Johnson v.2, p.314 (895)
134- Bancroft p.636 (733)
135- *Graphic* 9:26: 519 (1449)
136- *Columbian Gallery* (1599)
136 Inset- *Graphic* 9:26: 519 (1449)
137- *Das Columbische* (1603)
138- *Columbian Gallery* (1599)
139- Steinert p.25 (1536.1)
140- Steinert p.17 (1536.1)
141- Johnson, v.3, p.364 (895)
142- Underwood & Underwood Stereocard
143- Bancroft p.162 (733)
144- Kilburn Stereocard #8381
145- Shepp p.527 (1667)
146- Klein p.132 (902)
147- Shepp p.337 (1667)
148- *Graphic* 9.17: 331 (1449)
149- *Das Columbische* (1603)
150- *Columbian Gallery* (1599)
151- Bancroft p.815 (733)

152- *World's Fair Album* (1723)
153- *World's Fair Album* (1723)
154- Campbell 3.11: 313 (1462)
155- Campbell 3.7: 166 (1462)
156- *Reminiscences* (1660)
157- *Halligan's Weekly* 5.25: 588 (1324)
158- Shepp p.339 (1667)
159- *Reminiscences* (1660)
160- Johnson v.2, p.227 (895)
161- Johnson, v.2, p.232 (895)
162- *Das Columbische* (1603)
162 Inset- Silver coin, authors' collection
163- Johnson v.3, p.289 (895)
164- Scrapbook, authors' collection
165- *New England Mag.* p.561 (1368)
166- *New England Mag.* p.560 (1368)
167- Johnson, v.3, p.351 (895)
168- Jenks p.86 (20)
169- New York State. plate p.452 (1991)
170- New York State. plate p.468 (1991)
171- Bancroft p.172 (733)
172- Authors' photo of brass frame
173- *Pictorial Album* (1651)
174- *Gems of the WF* (1616)
175- *Columbus Outdone* p.163 (1050)
176- *WCE Reproduced* (1719)
177- Chromolith from program (1468)
178- Ropp. *W.F. Souvenir* (1662)
179- Ropp. *W.F. Souvenir* (1662)
180- *World's Fair Album* (1723)
181- *Halligan's Pictorial* (1623)
182- Bancroft p.273 (733)
183- Johnson, v.1, p.235 (895)
184- Johnson, v.2, p.253 (895)
185- *Pictorial Album* (1651)
186- Shepp p.271 (1667)
187- *World's Fair Album* (1723)
188- *Columbian Gallery* (1599)
189- *World's Fair Album* (1723)
190- Bancroft p.133 (733)
191- *Beautiful Scenes* (1575)
192- *Columbian Gallery* (1599)
193- Johnson, v.3, p.490 (895)
194- Campbell 3:12: 348 (1462)
195- Bancroft p.106 (733)
196- Shepp p.307 (1667)
197- *Reminiscences* (1660)
198- Shepp p.305 (1667)
199- Brass coin, authors' collection
200- Bancroft p.118 (733)
201- Johnson, v.3, p.499 (895)
202- Campbell 1.3: 21 (1462)
203- Campbell 1.1: 8 (1462)
204- *Pictorial Chicago* (1658)

205- *Pictorial Chicago* (1658)
206- *Pictorial Chicago* (1658)
207- *Gems of the WF* (1616)
208- *Pictorial Album* (1651)
209- *Pictorial Album* (1651)
210- *Columbian Gallery* (1599)
211- Bancroft p.140 (733)
212- Ropp. *W.F. Souvenir* (1662)
213- Bancroft p.143 (733)
214- *Graphic* 9.13: 246 (1449)
215- Bancroft p.131 (733)
216- Shepp p.25 (1667)
217- *Columbian Gallery* (1599)
218- Ropp. *W.F. Souvenir* (1662)
219- *Halligan's Weekly* v.5, part 23 (1324)
220- Martin (1630)
221- Martin (1630)
222- *Graphic* 9.2: 30 (1449)
223- *Graphic* 9.2: 30 (1449)
224- *Halligan's Pictorial* (1623)
225- Bancroft v.1, p.166 (733)
226- Bancroft v.1, p.214 (733)
227- *Das Columbische* (1603)
228- *Reminiscences* (1660)
229- *Pictorial Album* (1651)
230- *Harpers Weekly* p.485 (1314)
231- *Halligan's Pictorial* (1623)
232- Ropp. *W.F. Souvenir* (1662)
233- *Columbian Gallery* (1599)
234- *Pictorial Album* (1651)
235- Bancroft p.882 (733)

236- Bancroft p.841 (733)
237- Bancroft p.840 (733)
238- Authors' collection
239- Ropp. *W.F. Souvenir* (1662)
240- *Graphic* 9.10: 187 (1449)
241- Jenks p.60 (20)
242- *Graphic* 9.4: 63 (1449)
243- *Halligan's Pictorial* (1623)
244- Klein p.358 (902)
244 Inset- *Pictorial Album* (1651)
245- *Graphic* 9.10: 187 (1449)
246- *Columbian Gallery* (1599)
247- *Columbian Gallery* (1599)
248- Shepp p.501 (1667)
249- Shepp p.515 (1667)
250- Bancroft p.852 (733)
251- Johnson, v.3, p.440 (897)
252- *Columbian Gallery* (1599)
253- *Columbian Gallery* (1599)
254- *Pictorial Album* (1651)
255- Srail Columbian collection
256- *Halligan's Pictorial* (1623)
257- *Halligan's Pictorial* (1623)
258- Ellis p.334 (836)
259- Jenks p.78 (20)
260- *Graphic* 9.10: 186 (1449)
261- *Pictorial Album* (1651)
262- Klein p.350 (902)
263- Johnson, v.3, p.433 (897)
264- *Harpers Weekly* 37.1914: 805 (1314)
264 Inset- *Pictorial Album* (1651)

BIBLIOGRAPHY OF THE ILLUSTRATION SOURCES

Art and Artists of all Nations. New York: Bryan, Taylor & Co, 1894.

Bancroft, Hubert Howe. *Book of the Fair.* Chicago: Bancroft Co., 1893.

Beautiful Scenes of the White City. Chicago: Laird & Lee, 1894.

Campbell, J.B. *World's Columbian Exposition Illustrated.* Chicago: J.B. Campbell, 1891-94.

Columbian Gallery. Chicago: Werner, 1894.

Das Columbische Weltausstellungs-album. Chicago: Rand, McNally, 1893.

Ellis, John. *Chicago and the World's Columbian Exposition.* Chicago: Transcontinental Art, 1895.

Gas Engine & Power Co. *The Only Naphtha Launch.* Morris Heights, NY: The Company, 1893.

Gems of the World's Fair. Philadelphia: Historical Pub Co., 1894.

Graphic. Chicago: The Graphic News, 1893.

Halligan, Jewell N. *Halligan's Illustrated World.* New York: J.N. Halligan Co., 1894. [Cover title: *Halligan's Pictorial*].

Halligan, Jewell N. *Halligan's Illustrated World's Fair.* New York: J.N. Halligan Co., 1890-93. [Bannerhead: *Halligan's Weekly*].

Harpers Weekly. New York: Harpers, 1893.

Jenks, Tudor. *The Century World's Fair Book.* New York: Century Co., 1893.

Johnson, Rossiter. *A History of the World's Columbian Exposition.* New York: Appleton, 1897.

Kiralfy, Imre. *Imre Kiralfy's Grand Historical Spectacle America.* Chicago: I. Kiralfy, 1893.

Klein, Fred. *Unsere Weltausstellung.* Chicago: Fred Klein Co., 1894.

Kurtz, Charles M. *Official Illustrations from the Art Gallery.* Philadelphia: G. Barrie, 1893.

Lake Shore & Michigan Southern Railway. *The Lake Shore Route to the World's Fair.* N.p.: Cleveland Plain Dealer, 1893.

Martin, J.F. *Martin's World's Fair Album-Atlas.* Chicago: National Book & Picture, 1893.

New England Magazine. "Connecticut at the World's Fair." Vol.10. 1894.

New York State. *Report of the Board of General Managers.* Albany: J.B. Lyon, 1894.

Pictorial Album and History. Chicago: H.T. Smith, 1893.

Rand McNally & Co.'s Pictorial Chicago. Chicago: Rand, McNally Co., 1893.

Reminiscences of the Fair. St. Louis: Lester, Lawrence & Miller, 1894.

Report of the Massachusetts Board of World's Fair Managers. Boston: Wright & Potter, 1894.

Ropp, Silas. *The World's Fair Souvenir Album.* Chicago: Ropp, 1894.

Rose, H.B. *Harold and Carlton at the Columbian Exposition.* Hronellsville, NY: Times Assn, 1894.

Shepp, J.W. & D.B. *Shepp's World's Fair Photographed.* Chicago: Globe Bible, 1893.

Steinert, M. *The M. Steinert Collection of Keyed and Stringed Instruments.* New York: C.F. Tretbar, 1893.

Ward, Aretemas. *Columbus Outdone.* New York: Enoch Morgan's Sons, 1893.

The World's Columbian Exposition Reproduced. Chicago: Rand, McNally, 1894.

World's Fair Album. Chicago: Rand, McNally, 1893.

ADDITIONAL BIBLIOGRAPHY FOR THE CAPTIONS

Most caption information came from the above sources containing the illustrations. In addition, the following references were used for caption annotation:

Berry Brothers Ltd. *Description of the Mammoth Redwood Plank.* Detroit, MI: [Berry Brothers, 1893].

Condensed Official Catalogue of Interesting Exhibits With Their Locations in the World's Columbian Exposition. Moses P. Handy, ed. Chicago: W.B. Conkey Co., 1893. (1175)

Flinn, John J. *Chicago the Marvelous City of the West. 1892.* Chicago: Standard Guide Co., n.d. (1104)

Hale Elevator Co. *Elevator Tower To Roof of Manufactures and Liberal Arts Building.* [Chicago: Hale Elevator Co., 1893]. (862.3)

Official Catalogue : Part XVII. 1893 : of Exhibits on the Midway Plaisance. Moses P. Handy, ed. Chicago: W.B. Conkey Co., 1893. (1204)

The Official Directory of the World's Columbian Exposition. Moses P. Handy, ed. Chicago: W.B. Conkey Co., 1893. (1207)

California. *Final Report of the California World's Fair Commission.* Sacramento, CA: State Office, 1894. (1796)

INDEX

ABOUT THE AUTHORS

G. L. DYBWAD, RETIRED SOLID STATE PHYSICIST, HAS LONG BEEN A COLLECTOR OF COLUMBIAN EXPOSITION MEMORABILIA. JOY BLISS, RETIRED PHYSICIAN, JOINS HIM IN THIS AND OTHER BOOK ENDEAVORS. *WHITE CITY RECOLLECTIONS* IS THEIR SIXTH BOOK. NATIVE TO NORTH DAKOTA, THE COUPLE HAS LIVED IN ALBUQUERQUE, NEW MEXICO, SINCE 1990.